Pass AZ-900 Fast: The Ultimate Study Guide

Kameron Hussain and Frahaan Hussain

Published by Kameron Hussain, 2025.

PASS AZ-900 FAST: THE ULTIMATE STUDY GUIDE

First edition. May 21, 2025.

ISBN: 979-8231875924

Written by Kameron Hussain and Frahaan Hussain.

Pass AZ-900 Fast: The Ultimate Study Guide

First Edition

Preface

Cloud computing has revolutionized the technology landscape, and Microsoft Azure stands as one of the leading platforms empowering this transformation. Whether you're an IT professional looking to formalize your cloud knowledge or someone just beginning their journey into cloud computing, the Microsoft Certified: Azure Fundamentals (AZ-900) exam serves as an ideal entry point.

This book, *Pass AZ-900 Fast: The Ultimate Study Guide*, is designed to provide a comprehensive, structured, and clear path to passing the AZ-900 certification. It caters to absolute beginners while also benefiting professionals who seek an efficient way to reinforce foundational Azure knowledge.

The structure of the book reflects the official AZ-900 exam skills outline and expands upon it through the following chapters:

- **Chapter 1** introduces you to Microsoft Azure and provides an overview of the AZ-900 exam, its purpose, and its structure. It also explains how the certification can benefit your career.

- **Chapter 2** explores core cloud concepts, such as cloud computing principles, models (public, private, hybrid), services (IaaS, PaaS, SaaS), and the advantages of using the cloud.

- **Chapter 3** breaks down Azure's core services across compute, networking, storage, and databases, giving you real-world context for each category.

- **Chapter 4** delves into security, compliance, and trust, detailing the tools and resources Azure offers to meet regulatory and business requirements.

- **Chapter 5** focuses on pricing models, SLAs, and service lifecycles to help you understand how Azure supports operational and financial planning.

- **Chapter 6** is a practical hands-on section that includes guided labs and projects you can execute in your own Azure account.

- **Chapter 7** is dedicated to exam strategy, including reviewing measured skills, tackling trick questions, and optimizing your test-day performance.

- **Chapter 8** serves as a repository of additional materials including a glossary, code snippets, practice projects, and frequently asked questions.

Each chapter has been written to balance theoretical understanding with practical application, preparing you not only to pass the exam but also to apply Azure fundamentals in real-world scenarios.

Table of Contents

Chapter 8: Appendices

Glossary of Terms

A

B

C

D

E

F

G

H

I

K

L

M

N

O

P

R

S

T

Chapter 1: Introduction to Microsoft Azure and the AZ-900 Exam

Purpose and Audience of the AZ-900 Certification

The Microsoft Certified: Azure Fundamentals (AZ-900) certification is specifically designed to validate foundational-level knowledge of cloud services and how those services are provided with Microsoft Azure. Unlike role-based certifications such as Azure Administrator or Azure Developer, this exam does not require deep technical expertise or hands-on experience. It is ideal for anyone who wants to demonstrate a basic understanding of cloud concepts and Azure services, including:

- **IT professionals** exploring a move to cloud-based roles.
- **Sales and marketing professionals** supporting Azure-based solutions.
- **Business stakeholders** and decision-makers evaluating cloud platforms.
- **Students and beginners** looking to build a career in cloud computing.

This section will break down the purpose, benefits, and scope of the AZ-900 exam, and explain who should take it and why.

Why This Certification Matters

Cloud computing is no longer a niche skill—it is an industry standard. Organizations of all sizes are moving workloads to the cloud, and Azure is one of the top three cloud providers globally.

According to various industry reports, more than 95% of Fortune 500 companies use Azure in some capacity. By earning the AZ-900 certification, you prove your ability to engage in conversations about cloud adoption, solution planning, and basic service implementation.

The certification demonstrates that you:

- Understand basic cloud terminology.
- Can identify key Azure products and services.
- Know how pricing and support options work.
- Appreciate how Azure ensures security and compliance.

This foundational knowledge acts as a stepping stone for more specialized Microsoft certifications, including:

- **Azure Administrator Associate (AZ-104)**
- **Azure Developer Associate (AZ-204)**
- **Azure Solutions Architect Expert (AZ-305)**

Who Should Take the AZ-900?

While the AZ-900 exam is open to anyone, it is most beneficial for:

1. **Beginners in Cloud Computing**
   Those with no prior experience can use this certification as a launchpad.
2. **Business and Sales Professionals**
   Individuals involved in selling or managing Azure-based solutions will find the content relevant for understanding customer needs and product capabilities.

3. **Support and Helpdesk Staff**
   Having a solid grasp of cloud concepts can enhance the ability to troubleshoot and escalate issues effectively.
4. **Project Managers and Product Owners**
   Understanding the Azure ecosystem helps bridge communication between technical and non-technical teams.
5. **Students and Career Changers**
   For those entering the IT field, this certification provides recognized validation of essential knowledge.

How This Certification Benefits You

Career Advancement

Holding an AZ-900 certification can strengthen your resume and LinkedIn profile, particularly for roles involving cloud strategy, IT service management, and digital transformation. It serves as a signal to employers that you are cloud-aware and eager to grow professionally.

Organizational Credibility

If you're a consultant or business leader, this certification demonstrates that you can competently evaluate cloud service providers and align Azure services with business goals.

Entry into Microsoft's Certification Pathway

AZ-900 is often a required or recommended starting point for more advanced Azure certifications. Completing it builds familiarity with the exam process and content structure, making future certifications easier to tackle.

Broader Understanding of IT Trends

Topics like elasticity, high availability, scalability, and global distribution aren't just cloud buzzwords—they're essential components of modern IT infrastructure. The AZ-900 exam introduces you to these ideas in a clear and digestible way.

Common Myths About the AZ-900

Myth 1: It's Only for Technical People

Fact: Many candidates come from non-technical backgrounds. The exam is conceptual, and you don't need to write code or configure live systems.

Myth 2: You Don't Need to Study

Fact: While the exam is beginner-friendly, it still requires preparation. Azure services are numerous and nuanced, and understanding their differences takes effort.

Myth 3: It Has No Real Value

Fact: The certification is recognized globally and is a Microsoft-official credential that adds credibility and opens doors.

Skills You'll Learn

By preparing for this exam, you'll gain:

- A broad understanding of **cloud models**: public, private, and hybrid.

- Knowledge of **Azure services**, including compute, networking, storage, and databases.

- Familiarity with **Azure pricing models** and **cost management tools**.

- Awareness of **security, governance, and compliance features** in Azure.

- Basic hands-on skills in navigating the **Azure Portal** and setting up resources.

These competencies form a vital knowledge base whether you pursue a technical career or play a strategic role in your organization.

Learning Outcomes

By the end of this section (and the full exam preparation), you will be able to:

- Explain the core principles of cloud computing.

- Compare and contrast different cloud models.

- Identify core Azure services and describe their uses.

- Describe how Azure supports compliance and governance.

- Understand how to use the Azure Pricing Calculator and TCO tools.

- Be ready to sit and pass the AZ-900 exam confidently.

Sample Question

Here's a sample style of question you might see on the exam:

Question: Which of the following is a benefit of cloud computing?

A. Reduced energy consumption by user devices

B. Manual provisioning of hardware resources

C. Economies of scale

D. Limited geographic distribution of data centers

Correct Answer: C. Economies of scale

Explanation: Cloud providers like Azure serve millions of customers. This large scale allows them to offer more competitive pricing and efficient resource management.

Final Thoughts

The AZ-900 certification is more than just a test; it's an opportunity to build a strong foundation in cloud computing with Microsoft Azure. It prepares you for success not only in further certifications but also in modern roles that demand digital fluency. Whether you're pivoting careers or upskilling in your current position, this credential can set you apart and give you the confidence to speak the language of the cloud.

In the next sections, we'll begin exploring the world of cloud computing in depth, starting with what the cloud is, how it works, and why it matters today more than ever.

Exam Overview and Structure

The Microsoft Certified: Azure Fundamentals (AZ-900) exam is specifically crafted to assess a candidate's foundational understanding of cloud services and how those services are provided with Microsoft Azure. Unlike more advanced certifications, the AZ-900 exam is not designed to test deep technical skills. Instead, it focuses on conceptual clarity, basic practical knowledge, and the ability to evaluate Azure services in a business context.

This section provides a detailed breakdown of the AZ-900 exam's structure, the domains covered, question types, scoring criteria, registration process, and strategies for successful completion.

Exam Objective

The primary objective of the AZ-900 exam is to validate that the candidate possesses essential knowledge of cloud concepts, core Azure services, Azure pricing and support, and governance, security, and compliance features. It is not a prerequisite for any other Azure certification but serves as a solid foundation for advancing through Microsoft's certification hierarchy.

The exam is ideal for anyone looking to:

- Understand core Azure concepts before specializing.

- Engage in solution discussions with technical and non-technical stakeholders.

- Demonstrate cloud literacy in technical sales, project management, marketing, or procurement roles.

Key Exam Details

Feature	Detail
Exam Code	AZ-900
Name	Microsoft Certified: Azure Fundamentals
Duration	60 minutes (plus time for surveys and NDA)
Number of Questions	Typically 40–60
Question Types	Multiple choice, drag and drop, hot area, case studies
Passing Score	700 out of 1000
Cost	Varies by region (approx. $99 USD)
Languages Available	English, Spanish, Japanese, German, French, and others
Prerequisites	None
Validity	Does not expire (as of current Microsoft policy)

Domains and Weightage

The AZ-900 exam measures your understanding across several domains. Each domain is weighted differently, and knowing the approximate weight can help you allocate study time effectively.

Domain	Description	Weight
Describe cloud concepts	Covers benefits of cloud computing, types of cloud models, and types of cloud services	25–30%
Describe core Azure services	Overview of architectural components and core products	15–20%
Describe core solutions and management tools on Azure	AI, IoT, DevOps, and monitoring tools	10–15%
Describe general security and network security features	Azure's security mechanisms and best practices	10–15%
Describe identity, governance, privacy, and compliance features	Azure Active Directory, role-based access, compliance certifications	20–25%
Describe Azure cost management and service level agreements	Pricing calculators, cost optimization, SLAs	10–15%

These weights may vary slightly between exam iterations, but Microsoft publishes updated "skills measured" documentation that should always be reviewed before your test date.

Exam Format

Multiple Choice

The most common format. You'll often be asked to choose the correct answer from a list of four options. Some questions may require multiple correct answers (e.g., "Choose two answers").

Example:

Which Azure service is a Platform as a Service (PaaS) offering?

A. Azure Virtual Machines

B. Azure App Service

C. Azure Blob Storage

D. Azure ExpressRoute

Correct Answer: B. Azure App Service

Drag and Drop

These involve matching items, such as aligning services to their descriptions or models to their characteristics.

Example:

Drag each Azure service to its corresponding category (Compute, Storage, Networking).

Hot Area

This question type allows you to click areas in a diagram or user interface simulation. You'll often choose the right portal settings or features from a screenshot-like interface.

Case Studies

These are multi-question scenarios where you must analyze a situation and answer several related questions. Each question is based on the information in the case study and may not allow you to revisit previous questions once answered.

Example Question Set (Conceptual)

Question 1:

Which of the following benefits is associated with a public cloud model?

A. Enhanced security due to physical data center isolation

B. Complete control over the infrastructure

C. Economies of scale and reduced operational costs

D. On-premises compliance enforcement

Correct Answer: C

Question 2:

What is the purpose of Azure Resource Groups?

A. Group physical Azure servers

B. Deploy Azure services in multiple regions simultaneously

C. Manage billing across multiple subscriptions

D. Organize and manage resources as a single unit

Correct Answer: D

Registration Process

Registering for the AZ-900 exam is straightforward:

1. Go to theMicrosoft Certifications page[1].
2. Click on "Schedule Exam."
3. Sign in with your Microsoft account or create one.
4. Select your country/region to view pricing.
5. Choose an exam delivery option: **online proctored** (at home) or **in-person testing center**.
6. Pick a date and time, and complete the payment.

Scoring Methodology

The AZ-900 uses a scaled score system ranging from 100 to 1000, with 700 as the minimum passing score. The exam score is not a percentage; it reflects scaled performance relative to the difficulty of the questions you received.

Key facts:

- Each question has a pre-assigned weight.
- Not all questions are scored (some are used for calibration).
- No negative marking for wrong answers.

Microsoft does not disclose the exact algorithm, but consistent preparation across all domains is the best way to ensure success.

Retake Policy

- If you don't pass the first attempt, you must wait **24 hours** before taking it again.
- After the second attempt, there is a **14-day waiting period** before your next try.
- You can take the exam a maximum of **five times in a year**.

---

1. https://learn.microsoft.com/en-us/certifications/azure-fundamentals/

Exam Day Tips

- **Arrive Early (or Log In Early):** If testing online, ensure your room is secure, quiet, and free of materials.

- **Bring Proper ID:** Two forms of identification are usually required for in-person testing.

- **Test Your Equipment:** For online proctored exams, run the system check provided by Microsoft and ensure camera/microphone functionality.

- **Use the Break Wisely:** If permitted, take short mental breaks between sections.

Sample Preparation Timeline

Week	Activities
Week 1	Study cloud concepts and deployment models (25–30%)
Week 2	Learn Azure core services: compute, storage, networking (20–25%)
Week 3	Focus on identity, governance, security, and compliance (20–25%)
Week 4	Cost management, SLAs, hands-on labs, and practice tests

This timeline can be adjusted depending on prior experience and study hours per day.

Practice Labs and Resources

In later chapters, we'll cover full labs using the Azure Portal, but to complement your study now, you can:

- UseMicrosoft Learn[2]
- Practice with theAzure Pricing Calculator[3]
- Set up a free Azure account with £150 (or $200) in credit

```
# Azure CLI command to check current account context

az account show
```

Summary

The AZ-900 exam is a well-structured and accessible certification for anyone wanting to validate foundational Azure knowledge. The exam covers a broad set of cloud and Azure-specific concepts, providing a useful framework for deeper learning. Understanding its structure allows you to prepare smartly and target your study efforts efficiently. From learning how Azure services are categorized, to pricing tools and governance controls, each topic covered in the exam contributes to real-world cloud fluency.

In the next section, we'll dive into the key benefits of certification—why AZ-900 can make a difference in your career trajectory, how it aligns with modern IT trends, and what new opportunities it opens up.

Key Benefits of Certification

Earning the Microsoft Certified: Azure Fundamentals (AZ-900) certification is not just about passing a test—it represents a strategic investment in your future. In today's competitive technology landscape, certifications have become essential credentials that validate your skills, communicate your expertise to employers, and

2. https://learn.microsoft.com/en-us/training/azure/

3. https://azure.microsoft.com/en-us/pricing/calculator/

open new doors to opportunities across industries. This section will explore the broad and lasting benefits of achieving the AZ-900 certification, from personal development to professional growth, and how it aligns with industry trends.

Validation of Cloud Knowledge

One of the most immediate benefits of passing the AZ-900 is the validation of your foundational knowledge in cloud computing and Microsoft Azure. As organizations increasingly adopt cloud-based solutions, having a recognized credential confirms that you understand essential cloud concepts, including:

- Cloud models (public, private, hybrid)
- Deployment models (IaaS, PaaS, SaaS)
- Core Azure services (compute, storage, networking)
- Pricing models and service agreements
- Security, compliance, and identity management

Whether you're a beginner or someone transitioning into a cloud-focused role, this certification proves that you grasp the building blocks of the Azure ecosystem.

Increased Job Marketability

The job market has seen a significant shift toward cloud-centric roles. From developers and system administrators to sales engineers and project managers, cloud knowledge is increasingly in demand. According to reports by Gartner and IDC, cloud-related skills are among the fastest-growing skill sets across IT disciplines.

The AZ-900 serves as a differentiator on your resume or LinkedIn profile, especially for roles such as:

- Cloud Support Associate
- Technical Account Manager
- IT Project Coordinator
- Business Analyst (Cloud Focused)
- Junior DevOps Engineer
- Technical Sales Representative

By holding a Microsoft certification, candidates often receive more interview calls and are prioritized over non-certified peers, particularly for entry-level or junior technical roles.

Career Advancement and Role Mobility

AZ-900 is not just a standalone badge—it's the first step on Microsoft's cloud certification ladder. Successfully completing it provides a clear path toward more advanced and specialized certifications such as:

- **Azure Administrator Associate (AZ-104)**
- **Azure Developer Associate (AZ-204)**
- **Azure Security Engineer (AZ-500)**
- **Azure Solutions Architect Expert (AZ-305)**

With each step, your credibility, skill set, and value in the job market increase. AZ-900 acts as a launchpad, offering career mobility into more lucrative and strategic positions.

Many organizations have internal role-based ladders, and AZ-900 may qualify you for training budgets, internal promotions, or even cross-functional movements into cloud teams.

Alignment with Industry Standards

Microsoft certifications are globally recognized and vendor-approved. They're built and updated regularly based on industry needs, real-world application, and role-based requirements. The AZ-900, in particular, aligns with the skill sets defined in cloud industry frameworks like:

- **NIST Cloud Computing Model**
- **ISO/IEC 27001 Security Standards**
- **CSA (Cloud Security Alliance) Guidelines**

Employers know that certified professionals have been tested against an industry-aligned curriculum, ensuring consistency and trust in hiring.

Confidence in Professional Discussions

Another major benefit of certification is improved confidence. Whether you're in meetings with cloud architects, consulting with clients, or delivering presentations to stakeholders, being AZ-900 certified gives you the knowledge and terminology to:

- Explain Azure services and use cases
- Discuss cloud security and governance
- Understand pricing and cost control options
- Interpret cloud service level agreements

● Navigate the Azure portal with ease

This technical fluency improves collaboration across departments and enhances your influence in decision-making processes.

Competitive Edge in Non-Technical Roles

One of the unique aspects of the AZ-900 certification is that it caters to non-technical professionals as well. If you work in sales, marketing, finance, or operations within a tech-driven business, this certification can dramatically increase your effectiveness.

For example:

● **Marketing professionals** can better position Azure-based products.

● **Sales teams** can explain cloud benefits in client meetings.

● **Procurement officers** can evaluate cloud SLAs and pricing.

● **Executives** can make informed strategic decisions about cloud adoption.

By understanding cloud fundamentals, non-technical professionals can engage in more meaningful discussions with technical teams, reduce dependency, and accelerate project timelines.

Gateway to Hands-On Azure Experience

While the AZ-900 exam itself does not require deep technical skills, the learning journey often involves hands-on experience with the Azure platform. Microsoft provides free access through:

Activate Azure Free Tier account

az login

az group create—name MyResourceGroup—location eastus

az vm create—resource-group MyResourceGroup—name DemoVM—image UbuntuLTS

Creating and managing resources during your study gives you real-world experience. This hands-on exposure strengthens your understanding and makes the certification process more impactful.

Access to Microsoft Certified Community

Earning the AZ-900 certification grants you access to the Microsoft Certified Community—a global network of certified professionals, mentors, and employers. Community membership offers:

- Exclusive webinars and early product access
- Invitations to Microsoft events and conferences
- Digital badges for LinkedIn and resume display
- Recognition on certification directories

This network helps you stay updated, build your brand, and discover new opportunities for collaboration or employment.

Personal Satisfaction and Lifelong Learning

Beyond professional recognition, certification is personally fulfilling. It provides a structured learning path and a tangible goal that, once achieved, boosts your confidence and motivation. For many, it is the first step into a lifelong commitment to learning and continuous improvement.

Completing AZ-900 also encourages a mindset shift—from a fixed skillset to a growth-oriented, evolving IT professional ready to meet the changing demands of the cloud era.

Organizational Advantages

If you're part of an organization evaluating team certification, AZ-900 offers multiple business benefits:

- Accelerated cloud transformation by improving baseline knowledge
- Reduced dependency on external consultants
- Improved project outcomes through cloud-savvy staff
- Faster and more secure service adoption
- Enhanced credibility with partners and clients

Organizations that invest in foundational certifications like AZ-900 are better positioned to lead digital transformation initiatives, reduce cloud adoption risks, and optimize their Azure ROI.

Summary of Benefits

Benefit Category	Impact
Career	Improves job marketability, eligibility for promotions, and access to new roles
Skills	Validates core cloud and Azure concepts, builds foundational tech fluency
Confidence	Enhances technical discussions, cross-functional communication, and decision-making
Practical Exposure	Offers real-world experience with Azure tools and services
Community	Connects you with global professionals and learning resources
Business Impact	Empowers organizations to scale cloud adoption effectively

Final Thoughts

The AZ-900 certification is more than an entry-level credential—it is a strategic career investment. Whether your goal is to shift into cloud roles, advance your current position, or gain credibility in your industry, this certification delivers concrete benefits across professional and personal domains.

The learning journey that leads to certification builds the mindset and knowledge required to participate in the future of digital infrastructure. As we transition into increasingly cloud-native environments, holding a credential that confirms your ability to understand, evaluate, and work with Azure gives you a significant and lasting edge.

Next, we will explore how to plan your study effectively, manage your time, and take advantage of free resources and labs to ensure exam readiness.

Study Strategy and Time Management

Preparing for the Microsoft Certified: Azure Fundamentals (AZ-900) exam requires not only understanding the content but also approaching the preparation with structure and discipline. Many candidates, especially those new to certification exams or cloud computing, face challenges such as underestimating the material, poor time allocation, and lack of practical exposure. This section provides a comprehensive, actionable study strategy tailored to the AZ-900 exam, including study timelines, learning methods, tools, and time management techniques to help you confidently pass the exam on your first attempt.

Understanding the Scope of the Exam

Before building a study plan, it's essential to understand the breadth of the AZ-900 syllabus. The exam is broad but not deep—it covers multiple domains:

- Cloud concepts
- Core Azure services
- Azure solutions and management tools
- Security and network security features
- Identity, governance, privacy, and compliance
- Azure pricing and service level agreements

While you are not expected to implement or administer these services, you need to understand what they are, when they are used, and why they matter.

Setting Goals and Milestones

Start by setting a clear goal and defining your timeline. The average candidate typically requires 2 to 4 weeks of preparation, depending on prior experience. Here's a sample high-effort plan assuming 2 hours of study per day:

Week	Focus Area	Milestone
Week 1	Cloud Concepts, Core Azure Services	Complete 30% of the Microsoft Learn AZ-900 path
Week 2	Identity, Security, Compliance, Pricing	Complete 100% of the Microsoft Learn AZ-900 path
Week 3	Hands-on Labs, Case Studies, Practice Tests	Deploy sample services, complete 3 full mock exams
Week 4	Review and Reinforce	Focus on weak areas, finalize exam registration

Choosing Study Resources

Here are the essential resources recommended for exam success:

- **Microsoft Learn for AZ-900**: Official, free learning path. Highly interactive.

- **Exam Ref AZ-900 Microsoft Azure Fundamentals (by Microsoft Press)**: Detailed explanations aligned with the skills measured.

- **Udemy or Pluralsight Courses**: Look for updated courses that include labs and quizzes.

• **Practice Tests**: Use MeasureUp (official), Whizlabs, or Tutorials Dojo.

• **Azure Free Account**: Provides $200 of credits for one month and limited always-free services for hands-on practice.

Active vs Passive Learning

Understanding the difference between active and passive learning will boost the efficiency of your study sessions.

Learning Style	Examples	Retention Rate
Passive	Watching videos, reading blogs	Low to moderate
Active	Taking notes, doing labs, quizzes	High

Aim to engage with content actively:

• Take handwritten or digital notes.

• Rephrase definitions in your own words.

• Build small projects on Azure Portal (e.g., deploy a VM or create a storage account).

• Explain concepts aloud to yourself or others.

• Use flashcards for quick revision.

Sample Flashcards

Question	Answer
What is Azure Resource Group?	A container that holds related resources for an Azure solution.
What is PaaS?	Platform as a Service - a cloud model offering hardware and software tools over the internet.
What does Azure Active Directory provide?	Identity and access management as a service.
Name two pricing calculators Azure provides.	Pricing Calculator, TCO Calculator.

Creating a Study Environment

Your physical and digital environment greatly affects productivity. Ensure you have:

- A quiet, comfortable workspace.
- Reliable internet access.
- Distraction-free time blocks (use Focus Mode on devices).
- A structured folder system to organize study material.

Sample digital folder layout:

/AZ-900-Prep

/Notes

/PracticeTests

/AzureLabs

/ReferencePDFs

You can use OneNote, Notion, or Evernote to track notes and concepts across domains.

Example Daily Study Plan (2 hours/day)

Time	Task
00:00 - 00:15	Review flashcards from previous session
00:15 - 00:45	Watch or read new material on a topic
00:45 - 01:15	Take notes and summarize the topic
01:15 - 01:45	Perform related task in Azure Portal
01:45 - 02:00	Take a short practice quiz on the topic

Sample Hands-On Activities

Practical exposure to Azure is one of the most effective ways to reinforce what you learn. Some tasks you can perform using the Azure Portal or Azure CLI include:

```
# Create a resource group

az group create—name AZ900-Group—location westus

# Deploy a virtual machine

az vm create \

—resource-group AZ900-Group \

—name AZ900VM \

—image UbuntuLTS \

—admin-username azureuser \
```

```
—generate-ssh-keys

# Create a storage account

az storage account create \

—name az900storageacct \

—resource-group AZ900-Group \

—location westus \

—sku Standard_LRS
```

Try to:

- Deploy a VM and access it via SSH
- Create and manage a blob storage container
- Add a web app and configure it for deployment

Time Management Techniques

When preparing for the AZ-900, it's easy to either burn out or fall behind. Use these techniques to manage time effectively:

- **Pomodoro Technique**: 25 minutes focus + 5 minutes rest
- **Eisenhower Matrix**: Prioritize tasks by urgency and importance
- **Time Blocking**: Allocate calendar slots for studying to avoid overlap with work/personal life
- **Weekly Reviews**: At the end of each week, assess what topics you've mastered and where you need to reinforce.

Practice Test Strategy

Mock exams are crucial to success. Here's how to approach them:

- Use official-style exams under exam-like conditions (timed, no distractions).

- After each test, review every question—right and wrong.

- Use wrong answers to identify weak areas and revisit those topics.

- Do not memorize questions; focus on understanding the logic.

Practice tests also help you build mental endurance. Many candidates struggle with maintaining concentration for the full exam duration—mock tests train this skill.

Retention and Final Revision

In the final week before your exam:

- Revisit your notes and flashcards.

- Focus on high-weight domains (e.g., Cloud Concepts, Security, and Pricing).

- Take one full-length test daily if possible.

- Avoid cramming—give your brain recovery time.

Create a one-pager "cheat sheet" summarizing key definitions, tools, pricing models, and common services. Review it every day for 10–15 minutes.

Example entries:

Concept	Summary
Azure Region	A set of data centers deployed within a latency-defined perimeter
Azure SLA	Specifies the guaranteed uptime or performance for a service
Azure Cost Management	Tool to track and optimize spending across services

Common Mistakes to Avoid

- **Skipping practice labs**: Theory without practice reduces retention.

- **Cramming too close to the exam date**: Causes stress and confusion.

- **Ignoring low-weight domains**: Every point counts—neglecting small sections can cost a pass.

- **Not reviewing Microsoft's "Skills Measured" page**: This is your syllabus—study it directly.

Summary Checklist

- Registered for Microsoft Learn and tracked your learning path

- Created and organized notes with active recall techniques

- Performed hands-on labs in Azure Portal or CLI

- Completed at least 3–5 full-length practice tests

- Developed a daily and weekly study schedule

- Identified and improved weak topic areas

- Built a final one-page cheat sheet for revision

Final Thoughts

Effective preparation for the AZ-900 exam is not about reading vast quantities of information—it's about structured learning, regular practice, and consistent reinforcement. By managing your time wisely and engaging with multiple learning modes, you will not only pass the exam but also gain lasting foundational knowledge applicable in your IT career.

In the next chapter, we'll dive deep into the heart of cloud computing—its core concepts, models, and service categories—so that you understand why the cloud has become the default paradigm for modern IT infrastructure.

Chapter 2: Core Cloud Concepts

Understanding Cloud Computing

Cloud computing is a transformative model for delivering IT services over the internet on a pay-as-you-go basis. Rather than relying on local servers or personal devices for data storage and application execution, cloud computing enables organizations and individuals to access computing resources such as servers, storage, databases, networking, software, and analytics through remote data centers maintained by cloud providers like Microsoft Azure.

Understanding cloud computing is fundamental to succeeding in the AZ-900 exam and, more importantly, to navigating today's technology-driven environment. This section explores the definition, characteristics, service delivery, deployment models, and benefits of cloud computing, emphasizing how Azure enables these capabilities.

Defining Cloud Computing

The National Institute of Standards and Technology (NIST) defines cloud computing as:

"A model for enabling ubiquitous, convenient, on-demand network access to a shared pool of configurable computing resources... that can be rapidly provisioned and released with minimal management effort or service provider interaction."

This definition highlights key concepts:

- **Ubiquitous access**: Accessible anytime, from anywhere.

- **Shared resources**: Multi-tenant architecture supporting scalability and cost-efficiency.
- **Rapid provisioning**: Quick setup and teardown of services.
- **Minimal management**: Users focus on usage, not infrastructure.

Essential Characteristics of Cloud Computing

Understanding the core characteristics of cloud computing is vital. Azure, like other cloud providers, exhibits these traits:

1. **On-Demand Self-Service**
   Users can provision resources like storage and compute power without human interaction from the service provider.
2. **Broad Network Access**
   Services are available over the network and accessed through standard mechanisms, such as HTTP or HTTPS, enabling diverse platforms like mobile phones, tablets, laptops, and desktops.
3. **Resource Pooling**
   Resources (e.g., compute, storage, memory) are pooled to serve multiple customers, dynamically assigned based on demand.
4. **Rapid Elasticity**
   Resources can be scaled up or down quickly, often automatically. To users, resources may appear to be unlimited and available at any time.
5. **Measured Service**
   Cloud systems automatically control and optimize resource usage by leveraging metering capabilities appropriate to the type of service (e.g., billing per second or minute).

These characteristics allow organizations to achieve greater flexibility, cost savings, and scalability in their IT operations.

Traditional IT vs. Cloud Computing

Aspect	Traditional IT	Cloud Computing
Infrastructure Setup	Manual, physical servers	Virtualized, automated
Scalability	Limited, slow to expand	Rapid, often automated
Upfront Costs	High CapEx (Capital Expense)	Low OpEx (Operational Expense)
Maintenance	On-premises teams	Provider-managed
Availability	Risk of single point of failure	High availability, built-in redundancy

In cloud computing, users shift from owning infrastructure to consuming it as a service, allowing for a leaner, more agile operational model.

Types of Cloud Services

Cloud services typically fall into three categories:

- **Infrastructure as a Service (IaaS)**: Provides virtualized computing resources such as virtual machines, networks, and storage.

- **Platform as a Service (PaaS)**: Offers a managed environment for application development and deployment.

- **Software as a Service (SaaS)**: Delivers software applications over the internet on a subscription basis.

Each service model removes varying degrees of management responsibility from the user.

```
# Example Azure CLI to create a VM (IaaS)

az vm create \

—resource-group MyResourceGroup \

—name MyVM \

—image UbuntuLTS \

—admin-username azureuser \

—generate-ssh-keys
```

Benefits of Cloud Computing

Cloud computing provides numerous advantages that drive its adoption:

- **Cost Efficiency**: No upfront hardware costs; pay only for what you use.
- **Scalability**: Dynamically adjust capacity based on demand.
- **Speed and Agility**: Deploy applications and services quickly.
- **Reliability**: High availability, disaster recovery, and backup built-in.
- **Security**: Advanced security features and compliance certifications.
- **Global Reach**: Deploy applications across multiple regions for performance and redundancy.

These benefits apply across industries—from startups to enterprises, government institutions to educational organizations.

Shared Responsibility Model

A crucial concept in cloud computing is the **shared responsibility model**, which defines which security tasks are handled by the cloud provider and which are the user's responsibility. The division varies by service type:

Responsibility	On-Prem	IaaS	PaaS	SaaS
Physical Infrastructure	User	Provider	Provider	Provider
Network Controls	User	User	Provider	Provider
OS and Application Patching	User	User	Provider	Provider
Application Security	User	User	User	Provider
Data	User	User	User	User

Understanding this model ensures that customers remain aware of what needs to be managed and secured on their end.

The Role of Azure in Cloud Computing

Microsoft Azure is a cloud computing platform and a suite of more than 200 products and services designed to bring new solutions to life. Azure supports all the essential characteristics of cloud computing and offers:

- **Compute services** like Azure Virtual Machines, Azure App Services
- **Networking services** like Azure Virtual Network, Azure Front Door
- **Storage solutions** like Azure Blob Storage and Azure Files
- **Data services** like Azure SQL Database and Cosmos DB

- **AI and Machine Learning tools** like Azure Cognitive Services
- **DevOps tools** like Azure DevOps and GitHub Actions integration

Azure offers a unified management portal, SDKs, REST APIs, and command-line tools for seamless integration into modern development and deployment workflows.

Elasticity and Scalability in Practice

Elasticity is the ability to automatically grow or shrink resources based on demand, while scalability is the system's capacity to handle increased workload.

- **Vertical Scaling**: Increasing the size of a resource (e.g., upgrading a VM from Standard B1s to D2s).
- **Horizontal Scaling**: Increasing the number of instances (e.g., deploying multiple VMs or containers behind a load balancer).

Azure features like **Virtual Machine Scale Sets**, **App Service Autoscale**, and **AKS Cluster Autoscaler** enable both types of scaling.

```
# Example: Enable autoscale on an Azure App Service Plan

az monitor autoscale create \

—resource-group MyResourceGroup \

—resource MyAppServicePlan \

—resource-type Microsoft.Web/serverfarms \

—name MyScaleSetting \
```

—min-count 1 \

—max-count 5 \

—count 2

Use Cases of Cloud Computing

1. **Web and Mobile Apps**
   Host scalable, globally available applications using Azure App Services, API Management, and Azure Functions.
2. **Data Storage and Backup**
   Use Azure Storage, Backup, and Site Recovery for disaster recovery and redundancy.
3. **Development and Testing**
   Quickly spin up development environments with Azure DevTest Labs.
4. **Big Data and Analytics**
   Process large datasets with services like Azure Synapse Analytics and HDInsight.
5. **AI and ML**
   Run machine learning models using Azure Machine Learning and Cognitive Services.
6. **IoT**
   Collect, process, and analyze data from sensors using Azure IoT Hub and Stream Analytics.

Emerging Trends in Cloud Computing

• **Serverless Computing**: Execute code without managing infrastructure (e.g., Azure Functions).

• **Edge Computing**: Run services closer to the data source (e.g., Azure Stack Edge).

• **AI-as-a-Service**: Integrate AI capabilities without building models from scratch.

• **Multi-cloud and Hybrid Cloud**: Combine Azure with other cloud providers and on-premises environments using services like Azure Arc.

Summary

Understanding cloud computing is the cornerstone of the AZ-900 exam and the foundation for a career in modern IT. Cloud computing delivers flexibility, cost savings, scalability, and global reach. Microsoft Azure enables organizations to adopt cloud computing seamlessly by offering a comprehensive platform aligned with industry needs.

Key takeaways:

• Cloud computing offers on-demand, scalable, and metered services via the internet.

• Azure supports IaaS, PaaS, and SaaS models, as well as public, private, and hybrid deployments.

• The shared responsibility model outlines who secures what across the service stack.

• Real-world applications of cloud computing span app development, data analytics, AI, IoT, and more.

In the next section, we will explore the various cloud deployment models—public, private, and hybrid—and analyze when and why organizations choose each.

Cloud Models: Public, Private, and Hybrid

Cloud deployment models define how cloud services are made available to users and organizations. Each model—public, private, and hybrid—offers a unique blend of cost efficiency, control, scalability, and security. Choosing the right deployment model is critical for aligning IT infrastructure with business objectives, compliance needs, and operational demands.

Microsoft Azure, as a leading cloud provider, supports all three models, enabling organizations to implement cloud strategies that best suit their specific contexts. This section explores each cloud model in depth, comparing their features, benefits, limitations, and use cases, along with examples and guidance on how they are used in real-world scenarios.

Overview of Cloud Deployment Models

Cloud deployment models define the physical location and ownership of the infrastructure that delivers cloud services. These models include:

1. **Public Cloud** – Services are delivered over the public internet and shared across multiple customers.
2. **Private Cloud** – Services are maintained on a private network, either on-premises or hosted, dedicated to a single organization.
3. **Hybrid Cloud** – A mix of both public and private clouds, allowing data and applications to be shared between them.

Each model provides different levels of security, control, and scalability. Organizations often adopt one or a combination of these models based on their technical requirements, regulatory environment, and business goals.

Public Cloud

Definition:

A public cloud is owned and operated by a third-party cloud service provider (such as Microsoft Azure, Amazon Web Services, or Google Cloud Platform) and delivers computing resources over the internet. In a public cloud model, the cloud provider owns and manages all hardware, software, and infrastructure, and users access services through a web browser or APIs.

Key Characteristics:

- Multi-tenant architecture
- Pay-as-you-go pricing model
- Highly scalable and elastic
- Maintenance handled by provider
- Broad access from internet-connected devices

Azure Public Cloud Examples:

- Azure App Service (PaaS)
- Azure Blob Storage (IaaS)
- Azure SQL Database (PaaS)
- Azure Functions (Serverless)

Benefits:

- **Cost-Effective**: No capital expenditures, only operational expenses.

- **High Availability**: Built-in redundancy and geographic distribution.
- **Rapid Deployment**: Services can be provisioned within minutes.
- **Latest Technologies**: Instant access to innovations like AI, ML, and DevOps tools.

Limitations:

- Less granular control over infrastructure.
- Data residency and compliance issues may arise.
- Security concerns in shared environments (though mitigated by strong provider controls).

Use Cases:

- Hosting websites and SaaS applications
- Dev/Test environments
- Batch processing or large-scale analytics
- Startups or businesses with limited infrastructure budgets

Private Cloud

Definition:

A private cloud is a cloud environment dedicated to a single organization, hosted either on-premises or by a third-party provider. The infrastructure is isolated from other tenants and may offer greater control, customization, and security.

Key Characteristics:

- Single-tenant architecture
- Greater customization and control
- Often hosted in the organization's own data center
- Requires in-house or contracted management

Azure Support for Private Cloud:

- Azure Stack Hub: Extends Azure services to on-premises environments
- Azure Stack HCI: Virtualized workloads in a local datacenter with cloud integration

Benefits:

- **Enhanced Security**: Dedicated hardware and network isolation.
- **Custom Compliance**: Easier to meet specific regulatory requirements.
- **Full Control**: Organizations manage all components, including OS and middleware.

Limitations:

- **Higher Cost**: Requires capital investment and maintenance.
- **Limited Scalability**: Constrained by local hardware and capacity.
- **Longer Deployment Time**: Custom provisioning and setup times.

Use Cases:

- Government agencies with strict data sovereignty laws

- Financial services with intensive compliance needs
- Enterprises requiring tailored configurations
- Organizations with legacy apps unsuitable for public cloud

Hybrid Cloud

Definition:

A hybrid cloud combines public and private cloud models, enabling data and applications to be shared between them. This approach offers greater flexibility, optimized performance, and compliance alignment while maintaining some infrastructure on-premises.

Key Characteristics:

- Workloads can move between clouds based on need
- Unified identity and access management
- Integrated security and monitoring tools
- Seamless networking between environments

Azure Hybrid Capabilities:

- **Azure Arc**: Manage resources across environments using Azure services.
- **Azure Site Recovery**: Backup and disaster recovery between on-prem and cloud.
- **Azure VPN Gateway**: Connect on-prem networks to Azure.
- **ExpressRoute**: Private, high-throughput, low-latency connection to Azure.

```
# Example: Create a virtual network gateway for hybrid connectivity

az network vnet-gateway create \

—resource-group HybridGroup \

—name MyGateway \

—public-ip-address MyGatewayPublicIP \

—vnet MyVNet \

—gateway-type Vpn \

—vpn-type RouteBased \

—sku VpnGw1
```

Benefits:

- **Flexibility**: Retain sensitive data on-prem while scaling workloads in the cloud.
- **Business Continuity**: Disaster recovery and backup without dedicated secondary sites.
- **Cost Efficiency**: Move non-critical workloads to cheaper public cloud infrastructure.
- **Modernization**: Gradual migration from legacy to cloud-native environments.

Limitations:

- **Complexity**: Requires integration across heterogeneous environments.

- **Management Overhead**: Must handle orchestration, identity, and networking across clouds.
- **Potential Latency**: Inter-cloud communication may introduce performance lag.

Use Cases:

- Retail chains maintaining local servers with cloud analytics
- Healthcare providers storing sensitive data locally but using cloud-based AI
- Enterprises modernizing legacy systems gradually
- Businesses with seasonal demand requiring burst capacity

Comparison Table

Feature	Public Cloud	Private Cloud	Hybrid Cloud
Ownership	Third-party provider	Organization or dedicated host	Mixed (public + private)
Cost Model	Operational expense (OpEx)	Capital + OpEx	Mixed
Security	Shared responsibility	Full control	Selective control
Scalability	Very high	Moderate	High
Customizability	Limited	High	Moderate
Compliance	Shared	High	High
Management Complexity	Low	High	High
Best For	Startups, test environments	Regulated industries	Enterprises needing both agility and control

Decision-Making Factors

When selecting a cloud deployment model, organizations must assess multiple factors:

1. **Compliance Requirements**: Certain industries (healthcare, finance, defense) have data handling laws that may favor private or hybrid models.
2. **Budget**: Public cloud is ideal for minimizing upfront capital costs. Private clouds require larger investments but offer granular control.

3. **Existing Infrastructure**: Organizations with significant on-prem investments may lean toward hybrid models.
4. **Scalability Needs**: Businesses expecting rapid growth or seasonal spikes benefit from the elasticity of public cloud.
5. **Risk Appetite and Security Posture**: For sensitive data or mission-critical systems, private or hybrid deployments offer tighter control.
6. **IT Expertise**: Public cloud reduces operational burden, while private clouds require experienced infrastructure teams.

Real-World Examples

- **Public Cloud**: A SaaS company deploys a global web application using Azure App Services and Azure CDN, scaling to millions of users without managing infrastructure.

- **Private Cloud**: A multinational bank uses Azure Stack Hub to run financial workloads in its own data center, meeting internal data sovereignty requirements.

- **Hybrid Cloud**: A hospital runs its EMR system on-premises but uses Azure Cognitive Services for image recognition and diagnostics, enabling advanced capabilities while preserving privacy.

Summary

Cloud deployment models form the architectural foundation for delivering IT services. Each model—public, private, and hybrid—offers distinct advantages depending on the use case.

- **Public cloud** provides agility, cost savings, and scalability.

- **Private cloud** offers enhanced control, security, and compliance.

- **Hybrid cloud** combines the strengths of both, allowing organizations to tailor solutions to their unique needs.

Microsoft Azure supports all deployment models through its integrated services and hybrid capabilities, enabling seamless transitions and unified management. Understanding these models is crucial for designing effective cloud strategies and succeeding in both real-world scenarios and the AZ-900 exam.

Next, we will explore the core service models in cloud computing—Infrastructure as a Service (IaaS), Platform as a Service (PaaS), and Software as a Service (SaaS)—and how Azure implements them to empower modern IT solutions.

Cloud Services: IaaS, PaaS, SaaS

Cloud computing is delivered through three main service models: Infrastructure as a Service (IaaS), Platform as a Service (PaaS), and Software as a Service (SaaS). Each model represents a different level of abstraction and responsibility, offering varying degrees of control, flexibility, and management. Understanding these models is essential for making informed decisions about cloud adoption, application development, cost optimization, and resource allocation. In this section, we'll examine each service model in detail, explore their features, compare their use cases, and provide examples of how Microsoft Azure enables these models in real-world scenarios.

Overview of the Service Models

Cloud service models determine what aspects of an IT solution are managed by the customer and what aspects are managed by the cloud provider. The continuum moves from IaaS, where the user manages most of the stack, to SaaS, where the provider handles everything.

Component	On-Prem	IaaS	PaaS	SaaS
Applications	✔	✔	✔	✖
Data	✔	✔	✔	✖
Runtime	✔	✔	✖	✖
Middleware	✔	✔	✖	✖
Operating System	✔	✔	✖	✖
Virtualization	✔	✖	✖	✖
Servers	✔	✖	✖	✖
Storage	✔	✖	✖	✖
Networking	✔	✖	✖	✖

Infrastructure as a Service (IaaS)

Definition:

IaaS provides virtualized computing resources over the internet. The cloud provider manages the physical hardware and virtualization, while the user is responsible for managing the operating system, middleware, runtime, data, and applications.

Features:

- Virtual machines with configurable CPU, memory, and disk
- Load balancers and virtual networks
- Storage options (disks, blob storage, etc.)
- Network security groups and firewalls

Azure IaaS Services:

- **Azure Virtual Machines**
- **Azure Load Balancer**

- **Azure Virtual Network**
- **Azure Disk Storage**
- **Azure Bastion**

```
# Azure CLI example: Create a virtual machine

az vm create \

—resource-group MyResourceGroup \

—name MyVM \

—image UbuntuLTS \

—admin-username azureuser \

—generate-ssh-keys
```

Benefits:

- Full control over the OS and installed software
- Custom configurations for complex environments
- Easy scalability and automation
- Ideal for lift-and-shift migrations

Use Cases:

- Hosting legacy applications
- Test and development environments
- Running enterprise software like SAP, Oracle
- Custom network appliances and VMs

Challenges:

- Requires in-depth IT knowledge
- Higher maintenance overhead compared to PaaS and SaaS
- User is responsible for patching, monitoring, and securing the VM

Platform as a Service (PaaS)

Definition:

PaaS provides an environment for developers to build, deploy, and manage applications without dealing with the infrastructure. It abstracts away server management, OS updates, and runtime patching, allowing developers to focus on application logic.

Features:

- Built-in scalability and availability
- Continuous integration and deployment (CI/CD) support
- Integration with development tools (GitHub, VS Code)
- Supports multiple programming languages

Azure PaaS Services:

- **Azure App Service**
- **Azure SQL Database**
- **Azure Functions**
- **Azure Kubernetes Service (AKS)**
- **Azure Web Apps for Containers**

```
# Azure CLI example: Create an Azure App Service Web App
az webapp create \
—resource-group MyResourceGroup \
—plan MyAppServicePlan \
—name my-unique-app-name \
—runtime "NODE|18-lts"
```

Benefits:

- Rapid application development and deployment
- Managed databases, caching, and integration services
- Automatic scaling and load balancing
- Lower operational complexity

Use Cases:

- Web and mobile app development
- API hosting and microservices
- Event-driven architecture (via Azure Functions)
- Serverless application models

Challenges:

- Less control over the environment
- Vendor lock-in concerns
- Certain configurations may be limited by the platform

Software as a Service (SaaS)

Definition:

SaaS delivers fully managed applications over the internet. Users access the software via web browsers, while the provider manages everything—from infrastructure to application delivery.

Features:

- Subscription-based or pay-per-use model
- Automatic updates and patches
- Multi-tenant architecture
- Accessible from anywhere with internet

Azure SaaS Examples:

- **Microsoft 365** (Word, Excel, Outlook)
- **Dynamics 365** (CRM and ERP)
- **Power BI**
- **Azure DevOps Services**
- **GitHub (Microsoft-owned)**

Benefits:

- No installation or maintenance required
- Seamless collaboration and accessibility
- Predictable cost models
- High uptime and reliability

Use Cases:

- Office productivity tools
- Email and communication (Exchange Online, Teams)
- Customer Relationship Management (CRM)
- Business analytics and reporting

Challenges:

- Limited customization
- Data ownership and residency concerns
- Dependency on vendor's uptime and data handling practices

Comparison Table

Feature/ Aspect	IaaS	PaaS	SaaS
User Control	High	Medium	Low
Provider Control	Low	Medium	High
Customization	Full	Application-level	Minimal
Scalability	Manual or scripted	Automatic	Built-in
Maintenance	User	Shared	Provider
Speed to Deploy	Slow	Fast	Instant
Cost	Medium-High (OpEx)	Medium	Low-Medium (subscription-based)
Best For	Lift-and-shift, flexibility	Development, CI/CD, APIs	End users, non-technical users

Real-World Examples

IaaS Example:

A software vendor migrates its legacy on-premise Windows Server applications to Azure Virtual Machines to eliminate hardware dependencies. They retain control of the OS and application stack but benefit from cloud scalability and redundancy.

PaaS Example:

A startup uses Azure App Service and Azure SQL Database to launch a global e-commerce platform. They leverage auto-scaling and deployment slots to manage releases without maintaining infrastructure.

SaaS Example:

An enterprise adopts Microsoft 365 to streamline internal communication, document collaboration, and meetings, eliminating the need for on-prem Exchange and SharePoint servers.

Choosing the Right Model

Choosing between IaaS, PaaS, and SaaS depends on multiple factors:

- **Level of Control Required**: IaaS offers the most control, while SaaS offers the least.
- **Development Effort**: PaaS allows development without infrastructure headaches.
- **Budget and Resources**: SaaS and PaaS reduce operational burden, ideal for smaller teams.
- **Compliance Needs**: IaaS or private PaaS may be preferred for strict compliance requirements.
- **Legacy Compatibility**: IaaS is suitable for rehosting legacy apps without redesign.

Many organizations adopt a **multi-model strategy**, using IaaS for custom VMs, PaaS for web apps, and SaaS for collaboration tools. Azure enables seamless integration across these models, providing unified monitoring, security, and identity controls.

Summary

The cloud service models—Infrastructure as a Service (IaaS), Platform as a Service (PaaS), and Software as a Service (SaaS)—offer distinct capabilities suited to different needs. Understanding the differences among them is essential for selecting the right tools, optimizing operational efficiency, and achieving digital transformation goals.

- **IaaS** gives maximum control but requires the most management effort.

- **PaaS** strikes a balance by abstracting infrastructure while enabling application development.

- **SaaS** delivers ready-to-use software with minimal effort and fast adoption.

Microsoft Azure supports all three models, allowing organizations to choose the best mix of control, agility, and scalability. In the next section, we'll explore the specific advantages of cloud computing within the Azure ecosystem and how it empowers organizations to innovate and scale with confidence.

The Benefits of Cloud Computing in Azure

Microsoft Azure, as one of the leading cloud service platforms, offers a wide array of capabilities that empower businesses of all sizes to innovate, scale, and operate with greater efficiency. While cloud computing in general offers numerous benefits, Azure specifically brings a unique blend of integration, global reach, service depth, security, and hybrid support. Understanding these benefits is key to appreciating why organizations are increasingly adopting Azure to fulfill their digital transformation goals.

This section explores the broad and specific benefits of cloud computing in Azure across multiple categories, including cost, scalability, agility, performance, global presence, developer productivity, security, hybrid capabilities, sustainability, and innovation enablement.

Cost Efficiency and Optimized Spending

Azure helps organizations transition from capital expenditures (CapEx) to operational expenditures (OpEx). This pay-as-you-go model significantly reduces the need for upfront investment in hardware and infrastructure. Azure also offers several tools to manage and optimize cloud spend.

Key Features:

- **Pay-per-use billing**: Only pay for what you consume.
- **Reserved Instances (RIs)**: Commit to a 1- or 3-year plan for major cost savings.
- **Azure Hybrid Benefit**: Use existing Windows Server or SQL Server licenses to reduce costs.
- **Cost Management + Billing**: Built-in tools to forecast, track, and control spending.

```
# Example: Use Azure CLI to list pricing information

az consumption usage list—start-date 2024-04-01—end-date 2024-04-30
```

Benefits:

- Aligns IT costs with actual usage

- Reduces overprovisioning and idle resources
- Helps predict and manage budgets with tagging and resource groups

Scalability and Elasticity

One of the most valuable attributes of Azure is its ability to scale resources on-demand. Whether it's vertical scaling (upgrading instance sizes) or horizontal scaling (adding more instances), Azure handles both automatically through services like Autoscale, Virtual Machine Scale Sets, and Azure Kubernetes Service.

Scalability Options in Azure:

- **Virtual Machine Scale Sets** for IaaS workloads
- **Autoscale in App Services** for web applications
- **Elastic Pools** in Azure SQL Database
- **Azure Kubernetes Service (AKS)** with Cluster Autoscaler

Benefits:

- Respond instantly to workload changes
- Ensure optimal performance during peak times
- Eliminate manual intervention for scaling

High Availability and Business Continuity

Azure is architected for high availability at every layer. With regional and zone-based redundancy, organizations can ensure business continuity even during unexpected failures. Azure provides built-in features for disaster recovery, backup, and load balancing.

Core Services:

- **Availability Sets** and **Availability Zones** for redundancy
- **Azure Site Recovery** for automated disaster recovery
- **Geo-redundant Storage** (**GRS**) for data resiliency
- **Traffic Manager** for global load balancing

Example: You can deploy a multi-region application using Azure Front Door for traffic distribution and Azure Cosmos DB with multi-region write capability for global data consistency.

Benefits:

- Reduce downtime risk
- Meet SLAs with built-in redundancy
- Enable automatic failover to secondary regions

Global Reach and Local Presence

Azure has one of the largest global infrastructures, with over 60 announced regions and multiple Availability Zones within each region. This geographic distribution helps organizations deploy services closer to their users, improve performance, and meet local compliance and data residency requirements.

Azure Global Infrastructure:

- Azure regions across North America, Europe, Asia, Africa, and more
- **Availability Zones** for fault isolation

- **Edge Zones** and **Content Delivery Network (CDN)** for low latency

```
# List Azure regions via CLI

az account list-locations—query "[].{Name:name, DisplayName:displayName}"—output table
```

Benefits:

- Improved latency and user experience
- Redundancy and fault tolerance
- Compliance with national and regional data laws

Speed and Agility

Azure provides a flexible environment where you can provision infrastructure or platforms within minutes. Developers can rapidly deploy environments for testing, development, and production without delays related to hardware procurement or manual setup.

Agile Tools in Azure:

- **Azure DevTest Labs** for fast test environments
- **Azure Resource Manager (ARM)** templates for repeatable deployments
- **Azure DevOps** and **GitHub Actions** for CI/CD automation

Benefits:

- Rapid time to market for new features
- Faster experimentation and iteration

- Reduced developer dependency on IT teams

Security, Identity, and Compliance

Azure is built on a foundation of security and trust. With more than 90 compliance certifications globally and investments in advanced security tooling, Azure enables organizations to meet even the most demanding regulatory standards.

Security Services:

- **Microsoft Defender for Cloud**: Threat detection and security posture management
- **Azure Sentinel**: Cloud-native SIEM
- **Azure Active Directory (Azure AD)**: Identity and access management
- **Azure Key Vault**: Secure secrets, keys, and certificates
- **Azure Policy**: Governance at scale

Benefits:

- Secure by design with multi-layered protection
- Built-in compliance frameworks (e.g., HIPAA, GDPR, ISO)
- Role-based access and fine-grained identity controls

Example: Azure AD B2C can be used to securely authenticate users across consumer-facing apps using social and enterprise identity providers.

Hybrid Capability and Edge Integration

Azure excels in hybrid cloud scenarios, providing seamless integration between on-premises infrastructure and the cloud. Azure Arc, Azure Stack, and Azure Lighthouse are designed specifically to unify hybrid and multi-cloud environments.

Hybrid Tools:

- **Azure Arc**: Extend Azure services to any infrastructure
- **Azure Stack Hub/Edge/HCI**: Run Azure services on-prem
- **Azure File Sync**: Mirror on-prem files to the cloud

Benefits:

- Consistent management and governance across environments
- Edge processing and disconnected scenarios
- Centralized policy enforcement and identity management

Example: A manufacturing plant processes telemetry at the edge using Azure Stack Edge and syncs results to the cloud for further analytics.

Sustainability and Environmental Benefits

Azure is committed to sustainability and energy efficiency. Microsoft has pledged to be carbon negative by 2030 and has already achieved 100% renewable energy in many of its data centers.

Sustainability Programs:

- Real-time carbon tracking in Azure
- Sustainable datacenter initiatives

- Circular centers for hardware recycling
- Water-positive and zero-waste goals by 2030

Benefits:

- Reduce your organization's carbon footprint
- Achieve corporate social responsibility goals
- Leverage sustainability reporting in cloud resource planning

Integration and Ecosystem

Azure integrates seamlessly with Microsoft's existing ecosystem—including Microsoft 365, Dynamics 365, and Power Platform—as well as with third-party tools and services. It supports open source technologies and offers SDKs, APIs, and connectors for virtually any platform.

Integration Highlights:

- Native Power BI connectors for analytics
- Azure Logic Apps and Event Grid for automation
- Azure SDKs in .NET, Java, Python, Node.js, and Go
- Deep GitHub integration for DevOps workflows

Benefits:

- Unified developer experience
- Extend apps with minimal effort
- Reuse skills across the Microsoft stack

Continuous Innovation

Azure constantly evolves to include the latest advancements in cloud computing, artificial intelligence, machine learning, blockchain, and more. Organizations benefit from early access to innovations without having to manage or install them.

Innovation Services:

- **Azure OpenAI Service**: Integrate advanced language models like GPT
- **Azure Machine Learning**: End-to-end ML lifecycle management
- **Azure Synapse Analytics**: Unified big data and data warehousing
- **Azure Cognitive Services**: Vision, speech, language APIs

Benefits:

- Faster adoption of new technologies
- Stay ahead of industry trends
- Build intelligent applications at scale

Summary

The benefits of cloud computing in Microsoft Azure are both extensive and impactful. Whether you are a startup looking for flexibility or an enterprise seeking performance, Azure offers a cloud platform tailored to your needs.

Key benefits include:

- **Cost optimization** with granular control and flexible billing
- **Scalability and performance** with global reach

- **High availability** and built-in redundancy
- **Security and compliance** at enterprise scale
- **Hybrid support** with deep on-prem integration
- **Speed and agility** in deployment and development
- **Sustainability** with environmentally conscious data centers
- **Innovation** with cutting-edge AI, analytics, and automation

Together, these advantages make Azure a compelling platform for businesses navigating the digital era. In the next chapter, we'll shift from conceptual foundations to the core services Azure offers—starting with its architecture, resource organization, and primary services across compute, storage, and networking.

Chapter 3: Core Azure Services

Core Architectural Components

Microsoft Azure's architecture is designed to provide reliable, scalable, and secure services through a unified global platform. Understanding the core architectural components is essential for anyone preparing for the AZ-900 exam, as these form the backbone of all Azure services. This section dives deep into the primary components that enable Azure to deliver compute, storage, networking, and identity services at scale. It explains how these pieces fit together, their individual roles, and how they contribute to the broader Azure ecosystem.

Azure Regions and Availability Zones

Regions are geographical areas containing one or more datacenters. Each region is a deployment boundary for Azure resources.

- Azure currently operates in over 60 regions worldwide.
- Examples: West Europe, East US, Southeast Asia.

Availability Zones are physically separate datacenters within a region. Each zone has independent power, cooling, and networking.

- Typically, each region has at least 3 zones.
- Zones ensure high availability and fault isolation.

Benefits:

- Deploy resources closer to end-users for performance.
- Design applications for high availability using zone redundancy.

- Meet data residency and compliance requirements.

List available regions

az account list-locations—query "[].{Region:name}"—output table

Resource Groups

A **Resource Group** is a container that holds related Azure resources. Every Azure resource must belong to one—and only one—resource group.

- Resources in a group should share the same lifecycle.
- Enables easier management, deployment, and access control.
- Supports grouping for billing and tagging.

Example: A resource group can contain a web app, its database, storage account, and virtual network.

Create a resource group

az group create—name WebAppGroup—location westeurope

Best Practices:

- Group by application or workload rather than resource type.
- Apply consistent naming conventions and tags.
- Use role-based access control (RBAC) per group for security.

Azure Resource Manager (ARM)

Azure Resource Manager is the **deployment and management framework** for Azure. It provides a consistent layer for managing infrastructure through:

- REST APIs
- Azure CLI
- Azure Portal
- SDKs
- ARM Templates

Key Features:

- Declarative deployment (infrastructure-as-code)
- Dependency resolution and orchestration
- Role-based access and policy enforcement
- Tagging and grouping

ARM Template Example:

```
{
"$schema": "https://schema.management.azure.com/schemas/2019-04-01/deploymentTemplate.json#",
"contentVersion": "1.0.0.0",
"resources": [
{
"type": "Microsoft.Storage/storageAccounts",
"apiVersion": "2022-05-01",
"name": "mystorageacctdemo",
"location": "eastus",
```

```
"sku": { "name": "Standard_LRS" },
"kind": "StorageV2",
"properties": {}
}
]
}
```

ARM templates are JSON files that describe Azure resources and their configurations. They support repeatable deployments and CI/CD pipelines.

Azure Subscriptions

An Azure **Subscription** is an agreement with Microsoft to use cloud services. It provides:

- Access to Azure products and services
- Separate billing and usage tracking
- Resource isolation and quota management

Subscription Hierarchy:

Level	Description
Management Groups	Container for organizing subscriptions
Subscriptions	Billing unit and security boundary
Resource Groups	Logical grouping of related resources
Resources	Compute, storage, networking, etc.

Multiple subscriptions are useful for:

- Isolating environments (e.g., Dev/Test/Prod)

- Delegating administrative control
- Managing billing per department or team

Azure Tenants and Azure Active Directory (Azure AD)

An **Azure tenant** represents a dedicated, trusted instance of Azure Active Directory (Azure AD). Every subscription is associated with a single tenant.

- Azure AD is the identity and access management service for Azure.
- Provides Single Sign-On (SSO), Multi-Factor Authentication (MFA), and device management.

Key Concepts:

- **Users**: Human accounts managed in Azure AD.
- **Groups**: Collections of users for permission assignment.
- **Applications**: Register apps for identity integration (OAuth, OpenID).
- **Service Principals**: Represent apps or automation tools with permissions.

```
# Create a user in Azure AD (requires admin privileges)

az ad user create \

—display-name "Dev User" \

—user-principal-name devuser@yourdomain.onmicrosoft.com \

—password "StrongPassword123!"
```

Azure AD is central to access control in Azure resources through **Role-Based Access Control (RBAC)**.

Resource Providers

A **Resource Provider** is a service that offers Azure resources. Examples include:

Resource Provider	Description
Microsoft.Compute	Manages VMs and scale sets
Microsoft.Storage	Manages storage accounts
Microsoft.Web	Manages App Services and Functions
Microsoft.Network	Manages virtual networks, IPs, and NSGs
Microsoft.Sql	Manages Azure SQL databases

Enabling a provider:

az provider register—namespace Microsoft.Web

Every time you deploy a new type of resource, Azure uses the corresponding provider to manage it.

Azure Marketplace

Azure Marketplace is a catalog of third-party solutions, services, and virtual machine images that can be deployed directly into Azure. It includes:

- Application frameworks
- Database appliances
- Security software
- Infrastructure automation tools

Benefits:

- Accelerates deployment
- Reduces setup and integration complexity
- Offers certified and vetted solutions

Marketplace items can be deployed through the portal or automated with ARM templates and Bicep.

Azure Tags

Tags are name-value pairs assigned to resources for organizing and tracking.

- Apply tags to resource groups, subscriptions, and individual resources.
- Common tag types: Environment, Owner, CostCenter, Project, Department.

```
# Add a tag to a VM

az resource tag \

—tags Environment=Production Project=CRM \

—name myvm \

—resource-group WebAppGroup \

—resource-type "Microsoft.Compute/virtualMachines"
```

Use Cases:

- Cost management and chargeback

- Resource organization and filtering
- Automation and lifecycle management

Azure Blueprints

Azure Blueprints enable environment-wide deployments that combine:

- Role assignments
- Policy definitions
- ARM templates
- Resource groups

They are ideal for deploying governed environments in regulated industries or enterprises with strict compliance needs.

Benefits:

- Automate the creation of compliant environments
- Consistency across multiple subscriptions
- Integrated version control and lifecycle management

Azure Management Tools

Azure provides a suite of tools for managing resources:

Tool	Description
Azure Portal	Web-based UI for managing resources
Azure CLI	Cross-platform command-line tool
Azure PowerShell	Scripting automation for Windows and cloud ops
Azure SDKs	Developer libraries for .NET, Python, Java, etc.
Azure REST APIs	Programmatic control for all Azure resources

Summary

The core architectural components of Microsoft Azure form the foundation of its ability to deliver secure, scalable, and globally distributed cloud services. Understanding these components is essential to navigate and manage the Azure ecosystem effectively.

Key Takeaways:

- Azure is built on a global network of regions and Availability Zones for high availability and resiliency.
- Resources are grouped into **resource groups**, managed through the **Azure Resource Manager**, and tied to **subscriptions**.
- **Azure Active Directory** provides identity and access management, while **tags**, **ARM templates**, and **blueprints** ensure operational consistency and governance.
- Management tools like the Azure Portal, CLI, and SDKs provide flexible interaction methods for users and automation.

With a solid grasp of these architectural fundamentals, you'll be well-prepared to deploy, monitor, and manage a wide range of Azure services, which we'll explore in greater detail in the following sections.

Key Azure Products and Solutions

Microsoft Azure offers a broad and expanding portfolio of cloud products and solutions that span infrastructure, application development, analytics, networking, artificial intelligence, security, DevOps, and industry-specific needs. Understanding the core offerings is essential for passing the AZ-900 exam and for being able to recommend or implement appropriate solutions in a real-world context.

This section explores the major categories of Azure services, highlighting key products, their capabilities, and how they support different organizational needs across modern IT environments.

Compute Services

Azure Compute services provide the processing power required to run applications and services. Whether you need virtual machines, containers, serverless execution, or managed platforms, Azure offers solutions for all scales and complexities.

Key Services:

- **Azure Virtual Machines (VMs)**

Infrastructure as a Service (IaaS) that lets you deploy Linux or Windows virtual machines on-demand.

Use cases: legacy app hosting, custom environments, disaster recovery.

- **Azure App Service**

Platform as a Service (PaaS) for hosting web applications, REST APIs, and mobile backends with built-in autoscaling and CI/CD integration.

- **Azure Functions**

A serverless compute service that automatically executes code in response to events.

Use cases: background jobs, event processing, IoT triggers.

- **Azure Kubernetes Service (AKS)**

Managed Kubernetes for deploying and managing containerized applications at scale.

```
# Deploy a Linux VM
az vm create \
—resource-group MyResourceGroup \
—name DemoVM \
—image UbuntuLTS \
—admin-username azureuser \
—generate-ssh-keys
```

Storage Services

Azure Storage provides durable, scalable, and highly available storage solutions for all types of data—structured and unstructured, persistent or ephemeral.

Key Services:

- **Azure Blob Storage**

Object storage optimized for storing large amounts of unstructured data like documents, images, and videos.

- **Azure Files**

Shared file storage accessible via SMB protocol.

Ideal for lift-and-shift scenarios and legacy systems.

- **Azure Disk Storage**

Persistent block storage for use with VMs.

- **Azure Archive Storage**

Low-cost, long-term storage solution for infrequently accessed data.

Use Cases:

- Web app media content storage
- Data backups and archival
- File shares for distributed teams
- Data lakes and big data workloads

Networking Services

Azure Networking services enable secure, reliable, and high-performance connectivity for Azure resources, users, and hybrid environments.

Key Services:

- **Azure Virtual Network (VNet)**

Provides isolated, private network environments in Azure.

Enables communication between Azure services and on-premises networks.

- **Azure Load Balancer**

Distributes incoming network traffic across multiple VMs or services.

- **Azure Application Gateway**

A layer-7 load balancer with web application firewall (WAF) capabilities.

- **Azure DNS**

Host and manage DNS domains and records with low-latency global resolution.

- **Azure ExpressRoute**

Establishes private connections between on-premises networks and Azure.

Hybrid Networking Example:

```
az network vnet create \
—resource-group MyResourceGroup \
—name MyVNet \
—address-prefix 10.0.0.0/16 \
```

—subnet-name default \

—subnet-prefix 10.0.0.0/24

Databases

Azure offers managed database solutions that cover all major data models—relational, NoSQL, in-memory, and distributed.

Key Services:

- **Azure SQL Database**

A fully managed relational database built on Microsoft SQL Server. Offers built-in high availability, backups, and scalability.

- **Azure Cosmos DB**

Globally distributed, multi-model NoSQL database supporting document, key-value, graph, and column-family data.

- **Azure Database for MySQL/PostgreSQL**

Managed open-source database services with high availability and performance.

- **Azure Synapse Analytics**

Integrates big data and data warehousing for complex analytical workloads.

Use Cases:

- SaaS applications requiring high uptime
- Global apps with low-latency data access

- BI and real-time analytics platforms

AI and Machine Learning

Azure provides a wide array of artificial intelligence (AI) and machine learning (ML) tools to help developers and data scientists build intelligent applications.

Key Services:

- **Azure Machine Learning**

A platform for building, training, and deploying ML models using tools like Jupyter, Python SDK, and AutoML.

- **Azure Cognitive Services**

Prebuilt AI APIs for vision, speech, language, decision-making, and more.

- **Azure OpenAI Service**

Access to powerful language models like GPT, enabling summarization, translation, chatbots, and semantic search.

Use Cases:

- Real-time translation in web applications
- Image recognition in healthcare apps
- Predictive analytics in finance
- Sentiment analysis in customer feedback systems

Internet of Things (IoT)

Azure IoT services help organizations collect, process, and analyze data from connected devices at scale.

Key Services:

- **Azure IoT Hub**

Central message hub for bi-directional communication between IoT apps and devices.

- **Azure IoT Central**

A fully managed IoT app platform with minimal configuration.

- **Azure Sphere**

Secure microcontroller solution for edge IoT devices.

- **Azure Digital Twins**

Model real-world environments using digital replicas for simulation and insights.

Use Cases:

- Smart building monitoring
- Predictive maintenance in manufacturing
- Agriculture automation systems
- Fleet tracking and logistics

DevOps and Development Tools

Azure supports modern software development practices through robust DevOps services and integrations.

Key Services:

- **Azure DevOps Services**

Provides version control (Azure Repos), CI/CD (Azure Pipelines), test management, and agile planning tools.

- **GitHub and GitHub Actions**

Integrated source control and workflow automation, with built-in Azure integrations.

- **Azure Resource Manager (ARM)** and **Bicep**

Infrastructure as Code (IaC) solutions for automated deployment.

- **Azure API Management**

Design, secure, and manage APIs at scale.

Use Cases:

- Automating application delivery pipelines
- Managing infrastructure via code
- Hosting secure developer portals
- Deploying serverless microservices

Monitoring and Management

Azure provides centralized tools to monitor, log, and manage performance, availability, and security across your cloud environment.

Key Services:

- **Azure Monitor**

Collects metrics, logs, and telemetry for proactive monitoring.

- **Azure Log Analytics**

Query and analyze logs from across Azure and on-prem environments.

- **Azure Application Insights**

Tracks app performance, exceptions, and usage patterns.

- **Azure Advisor**

Provides recommendations for cost, performance, and security optimizations.

```
# Enable monitoring on a VM

az monitor diagnostic-settings create \

—name "vm-monitoring" \

—resource "/subscriptions/xxx/resourceGroups/MyRG/providers/Microsoft.Compute/virtualMachines/MyVM" \
```

—workspace "/subscriptions/xxx/resourceGroups/MyRG/providers/Microsoft.OperationalInsights/workspaces/MyWorkspace"

Identity and Access Management

Controlling access and identity is fundamental to cloud security. Azure Active Directory (Azure AD) is the core service here.

Key Services:

- **Azure Active Directory (Azure AD)**

Identity and access management with SSO, MFA, B2B/B2C support, and device management.

- **Role-Based Access Control (RBAC)**

Assign permissions based on roles to enforce least privilege.

- **Azure Policy**

Enforce rules across resources for compliance and governance.

- **Azure Key Vault**

Securely store secrets, encryption keys, and certificates.

Use Cases:

- Centralized user access across Microsoft 365 and Azure
- Conditional access policies for security
- Secure app-to-app authentication

Industry-Specific Solutions

Azure offers targeted solutions tailored to specific verticals:

- **Azure for Healthcare**: HIPAA-compliant services for EHR, imaging, and data integration.

- **Azure for Financial Services**: Risk analytics, fraud detection, and high-frequency trading infrastructure.

- **Azure for Government**: Secure, compliant environments for government workloads.

- **Azure for Education**: Scalable LMS and student data platforms.

Summary

Azure's product and solution landscape is vast and continually evolving. Each service is designed to solve a particular set of challenges, and the true power of Azure comes from its ability to interconnect these services into robust, end-to-end solutions.

Key Takeaways:

- Azure Compute, Storage, and Networking form the foundation for all workloads.

- Azure databases and analytics tools support structured, semi-structured, and unstructured data.

- AI, ML, and IoT capabilities enable next-generation applications.

- DevOps and identity tools streamline operations and improve security posture.

- Vertical-specific solutions ensure compliance and domain-optimized performance.

Mastering these core products and their use cases will give you a comprehensive view of Azure's capabilities and prepare you to recommend and implement effective cloud architectures. In the next section, we'll take a closer look at Azure's compute services and how they power workloads of every scale.

Azure Compute Services

Compute is one of the foundational pillars of cloud computing, and Azure offers a comprehensive suite of compute services designed to handle virtually any workload—from simple web apps to large-scale distributed systems. Azure Compute services enable users to run applications, host backend processes, schedule tasks, and build microservices-based architectures with scalability, security, and global reach.

In this section, we will explore the core compute services provided by Azure, including Virtual Machines, App Services, Containers, Kubernetes, and Serverless Functions. We will discuss their capabilities, pricing considerations, use cases, and how to choose the right solution for your scenario.

Azure Virtual Machines (VMs)

Azure Virtual Machines are Infrastructure as a Service (IaaS) offerings that allow you to run Windows or Linux virtual machines in Azure. They provide complete control over the OS and configuration, making them ideal for applications that require custom environments or legacy support.

Key Features:

- Wide selection of VM sizes for general purpose, memory-optimized, compute-optimized, and GPU workloads.
- Support for custom images and third-party images from the Azure Marketplace.
- Built-in support for scaling with **Virtual Machine Scale Sets**.
- Integration with Azure Backup, Azure Site Recovery, and Azure Monitor.

```
# Create a basic Linux VM

az vm create \

—resource-group MyResourceGroup \

—name MyVM \

—image UbuntuLTS \

—admin-username azureuser \

—generate-ssh-keys
```

Use Cases:

- Hosting enterprise applications (e.g., SQL Server, SAP)
- Running custom scripts and configurations
- Migrating on-premises VMs ("lift and shift")
- Running development and testing environments

Azure App Service

Azure App Service is a Platform as a Service (PaaS) offering that allows developers to quickly build, deploy, and scale web apps, APIs, and mobile backends.

Key Features:

- Support for .NET, Node.js, Java, Python, PHP, and Ruby.
- Continuous deployment from GitHub, Azure DevOps, and Bitbucket.
- Built-in load balancing and autoscaling.
- Deployment slots for blue-green deployments.

```
# Create a web app using App Service
az webapp create \
—resource-group MyResourceGroup \
—plan MyAppServicePlan \
—name MyWebAppDemo \
—runtime "NODE|18-lts"
```

Use Cases:

- Web and mobile backend applications
- Business APIs and RESTful services
- Lightweight SaaS applications

- Multi-region deployments for low latency

Azure Functions (Serverless)

Azure Functions offer a serverless compute option where you run code without provisioning or managing infrastructure. The platform handles scaling, availability, and server maintenance.

Key Features:

- Supports C#, JavaScript, Python, Java, and PowerShell.
- Integrates with over 200 Azure and third-party services through bindings and triggers.
- Event-driven execution (e.g., HTTP requests, queues, blob storage).
- Consumption plan charges based on actual usage.

```
# Example of an HTTP-triggered function in JavaScript

module.exports = async function (context, req) {

context.res = {

status: 200,

body: "Hello from Azure Functions!"

};

};
```

Use Cases:

- Microservices and event-driven apps
- Real-time processing of data streams
- Cron-like scheduled tasks
- Lightweight REST APIs

Azure Container Instances (ACI)

Azure Container Instances allow you to run Docker containers directly in the cloud with minimal overhead, making it one of the fastest ways to run containers in Azure.

Key Features:

- No infrastructure management required
- Supports Linux and Windows containers
- Easily integrates with Azure Virtual Networks
- Billed per second

```
# Run a container in Azure

az container create \

—resource-group MyResourceGroup \

—name mycontainer \

—image mcr.microsoft.com/azuredocs/aci-helloworld \

—ports 80
```

Use Cases:

- Short-lived batch jobs
- Container experimentation and development
- Rapid prototyping
- Stateless applications and RESTful APIs

Azure Kubernetes Service (AKS)

Azure Kubernetes Service is a managed Kubernetes platform that simplifies deploying, managing, and operating containerized applications.

Key Features:

- Integrated developer tools (Azure DevOps, GitHub Actions)
- Auto-scaling and self-healing clusters
- Network policies and pod-level security
- Supports Windows and Linux container workloads

```
# Create a basic AKS cluster

az aks create \

—resource-group MyResourceGroup \

—name MyAKSCluster \

—node-count 3 \

—enable-addons monitoring \
```

—generate-ssh-keys

Use Cases:

- Large-scale microservices architecture
- Complex app deployments with service mesh
- DevOps-centric workflows
- Hybrid and multi-cloud scenarios

Azure Batch

Azure Batch enables parallel and high-performance computing at scale. You can run large-scale parallel and HPC applications efficiently in the cloud.

Key Features:

- Support for thousands of virtual machines
- Built-in job scheduling
- Integration with licensing for applications like Autodesk, MATLAB, and others
- Auto-scaling of compute nodes

Use Cases:

- Rendering and simulation
- Financial risk modeling
- Image and video processing

- Genomics and scientific workloads

Azure Dedicated Hosts

Azure Dedicated Hosts provide physical servers that host one or more Azure virtual machines. Your organization has full control over the server capacity and physical isolation.

Key Features:

- Hardware-level isolation
- Control over maintenance schedules
- Compliance support (e.g., Bring Your Own License)

Use Cases:

- Meeting compliance or regulatory requirements
- Licensing scenarios needing dedicated hardware
- Consistent processor and memory configurations

Azure VMware Solution

This service enables organizations to run VMware workloads natively on Azure. It allows seamless migration of on-premises VMware-based applications to Azure without refactoring.

Key Features:

- Fully managed by Microsoft
- Supports vSphere, vSAN, NSX-T, and vCenter

- Maintains operational consistency with on-prem tools
- Hybrid integration with Azure services

Use Cases:

- Lift-and-shift VMware workloads
- Disaster recovery environments
- Long-term hybrid architecture

Choosing the Right Compute Option

Requirement	Recommended Service
Full OS control	Azure Virtual Machines
Rapid web app deployment	Azure App Service
Event-based or scheduled code	Azure Functions
Quick container runs	Azure Container Instances
Orchestration of containers	Azure Kubernetes Service
HPC workloads	Azure Batch
Dedicated physical isolation	Azure Dedicated Hosts
VMware migration	Azure VMware Solution

Pricing Considerations

Azure compute services use a flexible billing model based on the selected service:

- **VMs**: Pay per second while the VM is running. Reserved Instances offer cost savings.
- **App Services**: Billed per instance and tier (Free, Shared, Basic, Standard, Premium).

- **Functions**: Charged by execution count, memory, and duration.
- **AKS**: Only pay for the underlying VMs; the control plane is free.
- **ACI**: Pay for CPU and memory per second.

Use theAzure Pricing Calculator[4] to estimate and compare costs for compute services based on your workload.

Summary

Azure's compute offerings empower organizations to run a diverse range of workloads efficiently and cost-effectively. From full control of infrastructure with VMs to event-driven serverless functions, Azure provides flexible, scalable, and integrated options that fit modern application demands.

Key Takeaways:

- Azure Virtual Machines offer maximum control and compatibility for legacy workloads.
- App Service and Functions simplify deployment with managed environments and serverless execution.
- Containers and Kubernetes enable modern, portable, and scalable architectures.
- Batch and Dedicated Hosts support specialized and compliance-driven workloads.

By mastering these compute services, you'll gain the knowledge needed to design, build, and manage scalable applications on Azure. In the next section, we will explore Azure's networking capabilities,

4. https://azure.microsoft.com/en-us/pricing/calculator/

which form the backbone for secure, performant, and interconnected services across regions and platforms.

Azure Networking Services

Networking is the backbone of any cloud infrastructure. It ensures that services can communicate securely, reliably, and efficiently—whether they're within the same Azure region, across global datacenters, or integrated with on-premises infrastructure. Azure provides a comprehensive suite of networking services to support these needs, enabling the creation of scalable, resilient, and secure architectures.

In this section, we explore the core Azure networking services, their components, use cases, configuration patterns, and best practices for building connected systems in the cloud.

Azure Virtual Network (VNet)

Azure Virtual Network (VNet) is the fundamental building block for private networking in Azure. It allows resources like virtual machines (VMs), containers, and databases to securely communicate with each other, with the internet, and with on-premises networks.

Key Features:

- IP address space allocation (CIDR notation)
- Subnets for segmenting networks
- Integration with Azure DNS and custom DNS servers
- Support for routing, peering, and service endpoints

Create a virtual network with a subnet

```
az network vnet create \
—name MyVNet \
—resource-group MyResourceGroup \
—address-prefix 10.0.0.0/16 \
—subnet-name MySubnet \
—subnet-prefix 10.0.1.0/24
```

Use Cases:

- Isolating workloads
- Internal communication between services
- Hosting virtual appliances and firewalls
- Connecting hybrid environments

Network Security Groups (NSGs)

Network Security Groups control inbound and outbound traffic at the subnet or network interface level. They act as a firewall within Azure's virtual network.

Key Concepts:

- Rules are evaluated in priority order.
- Rules define source/destination, port, and protocol.
- NSGs can be associated with subnets or individual NICs.

```
# Allow HTTP inbound traffic
```

```
az network nsg rule create \
—resource-group MyResourceGroup \
—nsg-name MyNSG \
—name AllowHTTP \
—protocol Tcp \
—direction Inbound \
—priority 100 \
—source-address-prefix '*' \
—source-port-range '*' \
—destination-address-prefix '*' \
—destination-port-range 80 \
—access Allow
```

Azure Load Balancer

Azure Load Balancer is a Layer 4 (TCP, UDP) load balancing service that distributes traffic across multiple backend VMs or services.

Types:

- **Public Load Balancer**: Distributes incoming internet traffic.
- **Internal Load Balancer**: Handles traffic within a virtual network.

Features:

- Health probes for automatic failover
- Session persistence (optional)
- High availability with zone redundancy

Use Cases:

- Distributing web traffic across app servers
- Load balancing across availability zones
- Providing failover for stateful apps

Azure Application Gateway

Azure Application Gateway is a Layer 7 HTTP/HTTPS load balancer. It includes advanced routing and security features like Web Application Firewall (WAF).

Key Features:

- URL path-based routing
- SSL termination and end-to-end TLS
- Session affinity and cookie-based routing
- Autoscaling with zone redundancy

Web Application Firewall (WAF) helps protect against common web attacks like SQL injection, cross-site scripting, and more.

Use Cases:

- Routing requests to different apps based on path
- Hosting multiple web apps under one domain
- Protecting applications with WAF rules
- Handling SSL offloading

Azure Front Door

Azure Front Door is a global entry point that optimizes web traffic with intelligent routing, SSL offload, and global load balancing.

Key Features:

- Layer 7 HTTP/HTTPS load balancing
- Content caching (CDN integration)
- URL-based routing
- Custom domains and HTTPS

Use Cases:

- Accelerating global applications
- Building active-active deployments
- Enabling intelligent failover between regions

Azure Traffic Manager

Azure Traffic Manager is a DNS-based global traffic distribution service. It routes traffic to endpoints based on routing methods such as performance, geographic location, or priority.

Routing Methods:

- **Priority**: Route to primary unless it's unavailable.
- **Weighted**: Distribute traffic based on weights.
- **Performance**: Route to lowest-latency endpoint.
- **Geographic**: Direct users based on geographic location.

Use Cases:

- Multi-region web apps
- Disaster recovery failover
- Regulatory-compliant routing (e.g., data sovereignty)

Azure DNS

Azure DNS allows you to host your DNS zones and records in Azure using Microsoft's global infrastructure.

Features:

- High availability and low latency
- Custom DNS records (A, AAAA, CNAME, TXT, etc.)
- Integration with Azure Resource Manager and APIs

```
# Create a DNS zone

az network dns zone create \

—resource-group MyResourceGroup \

—name contoso.com
```

Use Cases:

- Managing custom domains
- Internal DNS for private resolution
- Automating domain management via Infrastructure as Code (IaC)

Azure ExpressRoute

Azure ExpressRoute provides private, dedicated, high-throughput connections between on-premises infrastructure and Azure datacenters.

Benefits:

- Higher reliability and security than VPN
- No data over the public internet
- Speeds from 50 Mbps to 100 Gbps
- Supports Microsoft peering and private peering

Use Cases:

- Hybrid cloud scenarios
- High-throughput, low-latency workloads
- Financial and healthcare industries with compliance needs

Azure Virtual WAN

Azure Virtual WAN is a unified network architecture that connects branch offices, on-prem environments, and Azure resources through a hub-and-spoke model.

Key Features:

- Centralized security with Azure Firewall
- Integration with VPN, ExpressRoute, SD-WAN devices
- Scalable architecture for large enterprises

Use Cases:

- Enterprise-wide network orchestration
- Secure and scalable connectivity between multiple sites
- Policy enforcement through a global transit network

Azure Bastion

Azure Bastion provides secure and seamless RDP and SSH access to Azure VMs without exposing them to the public internet.

Benefits:

- No need for public IP on VMs
- Encrypted access through the Azure portal
- Protection from port scanning and brute-force attacks

Use Cases:

- Remote administration of VMs
- Locking down VM access for sensitive environments

Azure Private Link and Service Endpoints

Private Link enables private access to Azure PaaS services over a private IP in your VNet.

Service Endpoints extend your VNet to Azure services without routing traffic over the internet.

Differences:

- **Private Link**: True private connectivity over a dedicated interface.
- **Service Endpoints**: Add a secure route within Azure's backbone.

Use Cases:

- Accessing services like Azure SQL or Blob Storage privately
- Avoiding exposure to public IPs
- Enforcing network security policies

Security and Monitoring

Key Tools:

- **Azure Firewall**: Stateful, cloud-native network security for controlling egress/ingress.
- **Azure DDoS Protection**: Automatic protection from Distributed Denial of Service attacks.

- **Azure Network Watcher**: Monitoring and diagnostics for network traffic and health.
- **Traffic Analytics**: Gain insights into network traffic patterns.

```
# Enable Network Watcher

az network watcher configure \

—locations "westeurope" \

—enabled true
```

Design Considerations and Best Practices

1. **Use NSGs and Azure Firewall together** for layered security.

2. **Choose Load Balancer vs App Gateway vs Front Door** based on layer and scale:

    - Load Balancer for TCP/UDP traffic
    - App Gateway for HTTP with WAF
    - Front Door for global routing

3. **Use Availability Zones** with Application Gateway for higher resilience.

4. **Isolate subnets** by role (web, app, database) for security and policy enforcement.

5. **Use Private Link for PaaS services** that process sensitive data.

6. **Implement logging** with Network Watcher and diagnostics to troubleshoot issues.

7. **Plan IP address space carefully** for long-term VNet scaling.

8. **Enable DDoS protection** for critical applications.

Summary

Azure Networking services provide the foundation for building scalable, secure, and highly available cloud solutions. From simple VM communication to complex global application delivery, Azure equips you with flexible tools to connect and protect your infrastructure.

Key Takeaways:

- VNets are core to Azure networking and support segmentation, isolation, and hybrid connectivity.
- NSGs and Azure Firewall enforce traffic filtering and protect internal assets.
- Load Balancer, Application Gateway, and Front Door offer various layers of load balancing.
- ExpressRoute and VPN Gateway support hybrid cloud strategies.
- Services like Private Link, Traffic Manager, and Bastion improve security, resilience, and operational efficiency.

A strong understanding of Azure's networking landscape is essential for designing robust cloud architectures and is a critical domain for success in the AZ-900 exam. The next section will focus on Azure's storage solutions and how they support modern data needs at scale.

Azure Storage Solutions

Storage is one of the most critical components of any cloud computing platform, serving as the foundation for applications, databases, analytics, media, backup, and disaster recovery. Microsoft Azure provides a rich ecosystem of scalable, secure, and high-performance storage services tailored for a wide variety of use cases. From object and file storage to disks, archives, and high-throughput data lakes, Azure's storage services are designed to meet the needs of both developers and enterprises.

This section explores the different types of Azure storage, including their architecture, features, usage scenarios, configuration options, and integration into broader Azure solutions.

Core Types of Azure Storage

Azure offers several core storage services, each optimized for a specific use case:

1. **Blob Storage** – Object storage for unstructured data.
2. **File Storage** – Fully managed file shares (SMB/NFS).
3. **Queue Storage** – Messaging service for distributed systems.
4. **Table Storage** – NoSQL key-value store.
5. **Disk Storage** – Block storage for virtual machines and containers.

These services are managed through **Azure Storage Accounts**, which serve as the top-level container for all storage services in a region.

Azure Blob Storage

Azure Blob Storage is Microsoft's object storage solution for the cloud, optimized for storing massive amounts of unstructured data such as documents, images, videos, backups, and logs.

Tiers:

- **Hot**: Frequently accessed data
- **Cool**: Infrequently accessed data (30+ days)
- **Archive**: Rarely accessed data (retrieval time hours)

Blob Types:

- **Block blobs**: For text and binary data.
- **Append blobs**: For logs and data that is frequently appended.
- **Page blobs**: For random read/write operations (e.g., Azure VMs).

```
# Upload a file to Blob Storage using Azure CLI

az storage blob upload \

—account-name mystorageacct \

—container-name mycontainer \

—name myfile.txt \

—file ./myfile.txt
```

Use Cases:

- Backup and archive

- Media streaming
- Data lakes and analytics
- Document and image storage

Azure File Storage

Azure Files provides shared file storage in the cloud using standard SMB or NFS protocols, enabling file sharing between multiple VMs or on-prem systems.

Features:

- Fully managed, serverless file shares
- Supports Azure File Sync for hybrid deployments
- Integrates with Active Directory (AD DS and Azure AD DS)
- Supports hot and cool access tiers

```
# Mount Azure Files share in Linux

sudo mount -t cifs //mystorageacct.file.core.windows.net/myshare /mnt/myshare \

-o
vers=3.0,username=mystorageacct,password=<account-key>,dir_mode=0
```

Use Cases:

- Shared file systems for applications
- Lift-and-shift of on-prem file servers
- User profile and data storage

- Hybrid file access via Azure File Sync

Azure Queue Storage

Azure Queue Storage provides reliable message queues for asynchronous communication between components in a distributed application.

Key Features:

- Highly scalable message queue
- Max message size: 64 KB
- Message TTL and peek-lock support
- Integrated with Azure Functions, Logic Apps, and custom services

```
# Add a message to a queue

az storage message put \

—account-name mystorageacct \

—queue-name myqueue \

—content "Hello from Azure Queue!"
```

Use Cases:

- Decoupling components in microservices
- Task scheduling and job queues
- Buffering user input for background processing

Azure Table Storage

Azure Table Storage is a NoSQL key-value store that supports rapid development of scalable applications.

Key Characteristics:

- Schema-less design
- Fast key-based access
- Optimized for large-scale datasets

Use Cases:

- Storing user metadata and app settings
- IoT device telemetry storage
- Log data and diagnostic info

Azure Table Storage can be an excellent fit for simple, lightweight applications that require fast reads and writes, and can tolerate eventual consistency.

Azure Disk Storage

Azure Disk Storage provides block-level storage volumes for use with Azure Virtual Machines and other compute services.

Disk Types:

- **Premium SSD v2/v1**: High IOPS and low latency for mission-critical workloads.

• **Standard SSD**: Cost-effective for web servers and lightly used enterprise apps.

• **Standard HDD**: Economical for infrequent access, backup, and archival.

Disk Capabilities:

• Managed and unmanaged options

• Encryption at rest with platform-managed or customer-managed keys

• Snapshots and backups

```
# Create a managed disk
az disk create \
—resource-group MyResourceGroup \
—name MyDisk \
—size-gb 128 \
—sku Premium_LRS
```

Use Cases:

• Boot volumes for Azure VMs

• High-performance transactional systems (e.g., SQL Server)

• Persistent storage for container workloads (via AKS)

Azure Storage Redundancy Options

To ensure data durability and availability, Azure offers several **redundancy options**:

Type	Description
LRS (Locally-redundant storage)	Replicates data three times within a single data center.
ZRS (Zone-redundant storage)	Replicates across three availability zones in a region.
GRS (Geo-redundant storage)	Replicates data to a secondary region for disaster recovery.
GZRS (Geo-zone-redundant storage)	Combines zone and geo-redundancy for maximum resilience.

Use GRS or GZRS when regulatory compliance or business continuity requires regional failover capabilities.

Azure Storage Security

Azure Storage provides robust security mechanisms to ensure data confidentiality and integrity:

Core Features:

- **Encryption at rest** using Storage Service Encryption (SSE)
- **Encryption in transit** using HTTPS endpoints
- **Customer-managed keys (CMK)** via Azure Key Vault
- **Shared Access Signatures (SAS)** for granular access control
- **Azure Defender for Storage** for threat detection and alerts

Create a shared access signature

```
az storage container generate-sas \
—account-name mystorageacct \
—name mycontainer \
—permissions rl \
—expiry 2025-01-01T00:00Z
```

Azure Data Lake Storage

Azure Data Lake Storage Gen2 is optimized for big data analytics, combining the scalability of Blob Storage with hierarchical namespace support.

Key Features:

- HDFS-compatible
- Seamless integration with Azure Synapse Analytics, HDInsight, and Databricks
- Fine-grained access control with POSIX-style ACLs

Use Cases:

- Big data pipelines
- Machine learning workloads
- High-volume telemetry and sensor data

Monitoring and Management Tools

Azure provides tools to manage, secure, and analyze storage usage:

- **Azure Monitor**: Track performance metrics and set alerts.
- **Storage Explorer**: GUI-based tool for managing Azure storage resources.
- **Azure Policy**: Enforce compliance (e.g., restrict non-encrypted storage).
- **Lifecycle Management**: Automate tiering and deletion of stale data.

```
# Example: Lifecycle policy JSON (auto-tier blob to cool after 30 days)
{
"rules": [
{
"enabled": true,
"name": "move-to-cool",
"type": "Lifecycle",
"definition": {
"filters": {
"blobTypes": [ "blockBlob" ]
},
"actions": {
"baseBlob": {
"tierToCool": {
```

```
"daysAfterModificationGreaterThan": 30
}
}
}
}
}
]
}
```

Cost Management and Pricing

Azure storage is billed based on the following dimensions:

- Storage capacity (GB per month)
- Operations (read/write/list)
- Data transfer out (egress)
- Redundancy and tier selection

Cost Optimization Tips:

- Use **cool/archive tiers** for infrequent access.
- Apply **lifecycle policies** to automate data management.
- Use **ZRS or LRS** instead of GRS if multi-region replication isn't required.
- Analyze costs using **Azure Cost Management** and **Storage Insights.**

Summary

Azure Storage provides a comprehensive, secure, and scalable suite of services for storing and managing data in the cloud. Whether you're building modern applications, running legacy workloads, or processing large-scale analytics, Azure Storage offers the flexibility and performance needed to support a variety of scenarios.

Key Takeaways:

- Blob Storage is ideal for object storage, with tiering for cost management.
- Azure Files supports traditional file-sharing use cases.
- Queue and Table Storage support asynchronous messaging and NoSQL apps.
- Disk Storage powers VM-based and container workloads with persistent volumes.
- Data Lake Storage enables high-throughput big data processing.
- Azure offers built-in security, redundancy, and management tools to optimize performance and compliance.

In the next section, we'll explore Azure's database offerings, including relational and NoSQL services, and understand how they support scalable, globally available data architectures.

Azure Databases

In modern application architectures, data plays a central role—whether it powers business transactions, fuels analytics, or enables real-time decision-making. Microsoft Azure offers a diverse and scalable range of cloud-based database services to accommodate virtually any workload, from small applications to globally distributed enterprise systems.

Azure's database services span relational, NoSQL, in-memory, and hybrid database engines. These services are fully managed, meaning Microsoft handles infrastructure, backups, high availability, patching, and scaling. This enables developers and businesses to focus on building data-driven applications without the burden of database administration.

This section explores the most important Azure database services, their use cases, architectural considerations, and features relevant to AZ-900 and real-world cloud adoption.

Azure SQL Database

Azure SQL Database is a fully managed, intelligent relational database service built on the Microsoft SQL Server engine. It supports both single database and pooled models, and offers high availability, scalability, and performance without requiring users to manage the underlying infrastructure.

Key Features:

- Serverless and provisioned compute tiers
- Intelligent query tuning and optimization
- Automatic backups and geo-replication
- Built-in high availability (99.99% SLA)
- Hyperscale model for large datasets (up to 100 TB)

Create a basic Azure SQL Database

```
az sql server create \
—name myserver \
—resource-group MyResourceGroup \
—location westus \
—admin-user adminuser \
—admin-password P@ssword123
az sql db create \
—resource-group MyResourceGroup \
—server myserver \
—name mydatabase \
—service-objective S1
```

Use Cases:

- SaaS applications with relational data needs
- Applications requiring transactional consistency
- Financial, HR, and ERP systems
- E-commerce platforms

Azure Database for PostgreSQL

Azure Database for PostgreSQL is a managed database service based on the open-source PostgreSQL engine. It supports both **Single Server** and **Flexible Server** deployment options.

Features:

- Advanced query capabilities with full-text search and JSONB support
- Built-in high availability with zone redundancy
- Custom maintenance windows and performance tuning
- Support for community extensions (PostGIS, pg_trgm, etc.)

Use Cases:

- Geospatial and GIS workloads
- Web and mobile backend storage
- Analytics pipelines
- Applications using open-source frameworks like Django or Rails

Azure Database for MySQL

Azure Database for MySQL is a managed MySQL relational database service offering scalability, availability, and secure connectivity.

Features:

- SSL enforcement
- Automatic backups and point-in-time restore
- VNet integration and private access
- Flexible Server for better performance control

Use Cases:

- Content management systems (e.g., WordPress, Drupal)
- LAMP/LEMP stack applications
- Open-source eCommerce platforms (Magento, WooCommerce)

Azure Cosmos DB

Azure Cosmos DB is a globally distributed, multi-model NoSQL database service designed for massive scale and low latency. It supports multiple APIs including:

- SQL (Core API)
- MongoDB API
- Cassandra API
- Gremlin API (graph)
- Table API (key-value)

Features:

- Guaranteed <10ms latency for reads and writes
- Global distribution with multi-region writes
- Tunable consistency levels
- Autoscale throughput
- Multi-master replication

Create a Cosmos DB account using the SQL API

az cosmosdb create \

—name mycosmosdbaccount \

—resource-group MyResourceGroup \

—kind GlobalDocumentDB \

—locations regionName=westeurope failoverPriority=0 isZoneRedundant=False

Use Cases:

- Real-time personalization and recommendation engines
- IoT telemetry ingestion and storage
- Global e-commerce and gaming platforms
- Serverless and event-driven applications

Azure Synapse Analytics (formerly SQL Data Warehouse)

Azure Synapse Analytics is a cloud-native analytics service that combines enterprise data warehousing and big data analytics.

Features:

- Integration with Azure Data Lake Storage Gen2
- Serverless SQL pool for ad-hoc queries
- Dedicated SQL pool for massive parallel processing (MPP)
- Deep integration with Power BI, Azure Machine Learning, and Azure Data Factory

Use Cases:

- Data warehousing and reporting
- Enterprise-scale analytics
- Business intelligence dashboards
- ETL pipelines and data modeling

Azure Cache for Redis

Azure Cache for Redis is a fully managed, in-memory data store based on the open-source Redis engine. It's used to accelerate application performance by serving frequently accessed data from memory.

Features:

- Millisecond latency
- High-throughput for read-heavy workloads
- Supports Pub/Sub messaging
- Geo-replication and Redis clustering

Use Cases:

- Session storage for web applications
- Leaderboards and real-time counters
- Message queues for event-driven systems
- Caching database queries and API responses

Azure SQL Managed Instance

Azure SQL Managed Instance provides near 100% compatibility with the latest SQL Server Enterprise edition, making it ideal for migrating on-prem workloads without code changes.

Features:

- Support for SQL Agent, linked servers, CLR, and more
- Built-in VNet support for secure connectivity
- Business-critical and general-purpose pricing tiers
- Automated patching, backups, and high availability

Use Cases:

- Lifting and shifting enterprise SQL Server databases
- Consolidating database servers
- Regulatory environments needing VNet isolation

Security and Compliance

All Azure database services come with robust security and compliance features:

- **Encryption at rest** using Transparent Data Encryption (TDE)
- **Encryption in transit** using TLS/SSL
- **Auditing and threat detection** via Azure Defender for SQL
- **Role-based access control (RBAC)** and **Managed Identities**
- **Private Link** and **VNet integration** for network-level security

- **Data masking** and **row-level security** for granular access

Example: Enable Advanced Threat Protection

az sql db threat-policy update \

—name mydatabase \

—resource-group MyResourceGroup \

—server myserver \

—state Enabled

Scaling, Backups, and Recovery

Scaling:

- Azure SQL, MySQL, and PostgreSQL support vertical and horizontal scaling.
- Cosmos DB scales throughput (RU/s) and storage independently.
- Synapse Analytics allows scaling compute nodes on demand.

Backups:

- Automated backups with point-in-time restore (up to 35 days)
- Geo-redundant backups for disaster recovery

High Availability:

- Built-in HA with zone-redundant deployments
- Failover groups for geo-replication

- Cosmos DB offers multi-region writes and 99.999% availability

---

Cost Considerations

Azure database pricing is influenced by:

- Compute resources (vCores, DTUs)
- Storage consumption
- IOPS and throughput
- Licensing model (pay-as-you-go, reserved instances)
- Features like geo-replication, backups, and autoscaling

Cost Management Tips:

- Use **serverless** or **flexible server** tiers for variable workloads.
- Implement **automatic scaling** to handle peak loads.
- Monitor usage with **Azure Monitor** and **Cost Management** tools.

Summary

Azure's database portfolio is designed to support diverse workloads, from traditional OLTP applications to globally distributed NoSQL systems and massive data warehouses. These services are fully managed, secure, and deeply integrated with the Azure ecosystem, making it easier to build, migrate, and scale data-driven applications.

Key Takeaways:

- Azure SQL Database and SQL Managed Instance provide scalable, relational databases for mission-critical apps.

• PostgreSQL and MySQL offer open-source relational engines in a managed cloud environment.

• Cosmos DB enables low-latency, globally distributed NoSQL data access with multiple APIs.

• Synapse Analytics supports data warehousing and big data scenarios.

• Redis Cache enhances performance with fast, in-memory data access.

With this knowledge, you'll be equipped to select the right database services for different business scenarios and prepare effectively for the Azure Fundamentals (AZ-900) certification. In the next chapter, we'll shift focus to Azure's powerful security, identity, and compliance features.

Chapter 4: Security, Privacy, Compliance, and Trust

Azure Security Tools and Features

Security is a foundational principle of cloud computing and one of the primary concerns for organizations moving to the cloud. Microsoft Azure addresses these concerns through a comprehensive set of integrated tools and services designed to protect data, applications, and infrastructure from threats. Azure security services are designed to operate at multiple layers—identity, network, compute, storage, and application—delivering defense in depth across all workloads.

This section provides an in-depth overview of Azure's security capabilities, tools, and best practices. These include built-in protections, monitoring and management tools, threat detection, vulnerability assessment, and governance controls. The goal is to help you understand how Azure implements and supports robust security frameworks to meet business and regulatory needs.

Shared Responsibility Model

In cloud environments, security responsibilities are shared between the cloud provider and the customer. This model ensures clarity about who is responsible for what.

Service Model	Provider Responsible	Customer Responsible
IaaS	Physical hosts, datacenters, networking	OS, applications, data, network config
PaaS	Infrastructure, runtime, OS, application stack	Data, access control, app logic
SaaS	Entire stack	Data and identity governance

Understanding this division is crucial. For example, Azure secures the hardware and core networking, but you must configure access policies, manage identities, and protect your data.

Microsoft Defender for Cloud

Microsoft Defender for Cloud (formerly Azure Security Center) is a unified infrastructure security management system that provides:

- **Posture management**: Identify misconfigurations and apply security recommendations.
- **Threat protection**: Real-time threat detection across Azure and hybrid resources.
- **Compliance management**: Assess alignment with standards such as CIS, NIST, ISO 27001, PCI-DSS, and more.
- **Secure Score**: A quantified metric showing how well your environment is secured.

```
# Enable Microsoft Defender for Cloud for a subscription

az security pricing create \

—name VirtualMachines \
```

—tier Standard

Use Cases:

- Detect brute-force attacks on virtual machines
- Identify unencrypted storage or open ports
- Alert on malware injection or anomalous activity

Microsoft Sentinel

Microsoft Sentinel is a cloud-native Security Information and Event Management (SIEM) and Security Orchestration Automated Response (SOAR) solution.

Features:

- Collects data from Azure, on-premises, and third-party sources
- Uses built-in machine learning to detect suspicious behavior
- Provides investigation tools with timeline reconstruction
- Enables automated incident response via playbooks (Logic Apps)

Common Data Sources:

- Azure AD logs
- Office 365 activity
- Network firewalls
- Endpoint protection platforms

Use Cases:

- Centralized security monitoring
- Threat hunting and correlation
- Real-time alerting and automation

Azure Firewall

Azure Firewall is a cloud-native, stateful network security service that allows you to centrally govern and log all traffic.

Features:

- Application and network-level filtering rules
- Threat intelligence-based filtering using Microsoft Threat Intelligence feeds
- Integration with Azure Monitor and Sentinel
- DNAT (Destination Network Address Translation) support

Use Cases:

- Enforcing egress/ingress control in hub-and-spoke network models
- Blocking known malicious IPs or domains
- Regulating access to SaaS platforms by FQDN rules

Azure DDoS Protection

Azure DDoS Protection provides automatic protection from volumetric, protocol, and resource (application layer) Distributed Denial of Service (DDoS) attacks.

Tiers:

- **Basic**: Included by default on all Azure services.
- **Standard**: Enhanced mitigation, telemetry, and logging. SLA-backed.

Features:

- Always-on traffic monitoring
- Adaptive tuning per workload
- Rapid attack mitigation
- Integration with Azure Monitor and Sentinel

Use Cases:

- Public-facing applications
- Financial platforms or critical APIs
- Applications deployed in virtual networks

Azure Key Vault

Azure Key Vault helps safeguard cryptographic keys, secrets, and certificates used by cloud applications and services.

Capabilities:

- Store secrets such as passwords, connection strings, and API keys
- Manage and control access to encryption keys
- Integrate with managed identity for secure access

- Support for Hardware Security Modules (HSM)

Create a Key Vault and store a secret

az keyvault create—name MyKeyVault—resource-group MyRG—location eastus

az keyvault secret set—vault-name MyKeyVault—name "DbPassword"—value "MySecureP@ssw0rd"

Use Cases:

- Centralized secret management
- Encryption key control for storage and databases
- TLS/SSL certificate management

Azure Bastion

Azure Bastion provides secure and seamless RDP and SSH connectivity to your virtual machines without exposing them to the public internet.

Benefits:

- No need for public IP addresses on VMs
- Fully managed PaaS
- Prevents port scanning and brute-force attacks
- Integrated with Azure Portal

Use Cases:

- Administering VMs in sensitive workloads

- Securing access to development and staging environments
- Locking down VM access in regulated environments

Just-In-Time (JIT) VM Access

JIT is a feature of Microsoft Defender for Cloud that restricts inbound traffic to virtual machines by requiring access to be explicitly requested and time-limited.

Workflow:

1. Admin requests access via the portal or API.
2. JIT creates a temporary NSG rule.
3. Rule is automatically removed after a defined period.

Use Cases:

- Reducing the attack surface
- Auditing and controlling administrative access
- Supporting secure remote operations

Security Best Practices

To ensure a secure Azure deployment, adhere to the following best practices:

Identity:

- Use Azure AD for all identity and access management.
- Enforce Multi-Factor Authentication (MFA).

- Use Conditional Access Policies to restrict access based on context.
- Leverage Managed Identities for secure app authentication.

Network:

- Isolate resources with Virtual Networks and subnets.
- Use NSGs and Azure Firewall to restrict traffic.
- Disable unused ports and protocols.
- Integrate DDoS Standard protection for critical apps.

Compute:

- Use JIT for VM access.
- Apply latest OS and app patches.
- Encrypt VM disks with Azure Disk Encryption.

Data:

- Use Azure Storage encryption with customer-managed keys when required.
- Store sensitive information in Azure Key Vault.
- Apply soft delete and immutable blob protection for backup integrity.

Monitoring:

- Enable Defender for Cloud across all subscriptions.
- Configure centralized logging via Log Analytics.
- Use Sentinel for correlation, detection, and automated responses.

Compliance Certifications and Trust Center

Azure meets a broad set of international and industry-specific compliance standards, including:

- ISO/IEC 27001, 27017, 27018
- SOC 1/2/3
- PCI-DSS
- HIPAA
- FedRAMP
- GDPR

You can explore certifications, audit reports, and regulatory compliance documentation through the **Microsoft Trust Center** and **Compliance Manager**.

Summary

Microsoft Azure provides a robust and integrated set of security tools that span all layers of the cloud environment—from identity and network to compute and storage. These tools help organizations enforce security best practices, protect against evolving threats, and demonstrate compliance with regulatory requirements.

Key Takeaways:

- Microsoft Defender for Cloud offers a unified view of security posture and threat protection.
- Azure Sentinel delivers advanced SIEM capabilities with built-in machine learning and automation.
- Services like Azure Firewall, DDoS Protection, and Bastion help enforce network security.
- Azure Key Vault centralizes secret and key management with tight access control.
- The shared responsibility model defines which security responsibilities lie with you.

By leveraging these services effectively, organizations can build resilient, secure, and compliant cloud environments on Azure. In the next section, we'll delve into Azure's networking security and access control mechanisms to see how data and traffic are protected at the infrastructure level.

Network Security and Access Control

In Microsoft Azure, network security and access control are essential to protect resources, enforce governance, and ensure that data is transmitted securely within and beyond the cloud. Azure offers a rich set of tools and services that provide layered protection—from virtual network isolation to perimeter defense and fine-grained access rules. This section explores the key components, configurations, best practices, and real-world applications of Azure network security and access control capabilities.

Defense in Depth: A Layered Security Approach

Azure's networking model follows the **defense in depth** strategy, applying multiple levels of security across an architecture. These include:

1. **Perimeter layer** – DDoS protection, Azure Firewall
2. **Network layer** – Virtual Networks, Subnets, NSGs, Route Tables
3. **Access layer** – Bastion, VPN, Private Link
4. **Application layer** – Application Gateway, WAF, SSL termination
5. **Data layer** – Encryption, key management, storage firewalls

Each layer complements the others, collectively strengthening security posture.

Azure Virtual Network (VNet)

A **Virtual Network (VNet)** is the foundational component for Azure networking. It enables secure communication between Azure resources, on-prem environments, and the internet.

Key Security Capabilities:

- **Subnet segmentation**: Separate services logically for isolation and access control.
- **Custom routing**: Use route tables to direct traffic through inspection or filtering services.
- **Service endpoints**: Extend VNet identity to Azure services for secure, direct access.

- **Private Link**: Access PaaS services over a private IP without traversing the public internet.

```
# Create a VNet with two subnets
az network vnet create \
—name AppVNet \
—resource-group MyRG \
—address-prefix 10.0.0.0/16 \
—subnet-name WebSubnet \
—subnet-prefix 10.0.1.0/24
az network vnet subnet create \
—vnet-name AppVNet \
—name DataSubnet \
—resource-group MyRG \
—address-prefix 10.0.2.0/24
```

Network Security Groups (NSGs)

Network Security Groups (NSGs) are rules-based firewalls that control traffic to and from Azure resources at the subnet or network interface level.

Key Features:

- Inbound and outbound rule definition
- Priority-based rule evaluation

- Default deny-all rule to enforce least privilege
- Support for service tags and application security groups

```
# Allow HTTP inbound to a subnet

az network nsg rule create \

—resource-group MyRG \

—nsg-name WebNSG \

—name AllowHTTP \

—priority 100 \

—direction Inbound \

—access Allow \

—protocol Tcp \

—source-address-prefix Internet \

—destination-port-range 80
```

Best Practices:

- Apply NSGs to both subnets and NICs for maximum control.
- Use **service tags** (e.g., AzureLoadBalancer, Internet, Storage) for simplified configuration.
- Use **application security groups (ASGs)** to group VMs by role and control communication between roles logically.

Azure Firewall

Azure Firewall is a fully managed, stateful firewall as a service that provides high availability and centralized logging.

Core Capabilities:

- Application and network rule sets
- Threat intelligence filtering with Microsoft threat feeds
- DNS proxy and filtering
- FQDN-based rules for outbound control
- Integration with Azure Policy for governance

```
# Example rule: allow outbound access to Microsoft.com

az network firewall application-rule create \

—firewall-name MyFirewall \

—resource-group MyRG \

—collection-name AppRuleCollection \

—rule-name AllowMS \

—protocols Http=80 Https=443 \

—target-fqdns www.microsoft.com \

—source-addresses 10.0.1.0/24 \

—action Allow \

—priority 100
```

Use Cases:

- Centralized egress filtering
- Enforcing corporate access policies
- Logging and monitoring traffic from all regions

Azure DDoS Protection

Azure provides **Distributed Denial of Service (DDoS) Protection** to guard against volumetric and protocol attacks that aim to overwhelm your applications or resources.

Service Levels:

- **Basic**: Always-on, included at no additional cost.
- **Standard**: Enhanced mitigation, telemetry, and SLA.

Features:

- Adaptive real-time tuning
- Logging and analytics integration
- Cost protection for scaling during attack

Best Practice: Use DDoS Standard with a Web Application Firewall (WAF) for complete L3–L7 protection.

Azure Application Gateway and WAF

Azure Application Gateway is a Layer 7 load balancer that enables secure application delivery with integrated **Web Application Firewall (WAF)** capabilities.

WAF Features:

- Preconfigured OWASP Core Rule Sets (CRS)
- SQL injection and XSS protection
- Custom rules and rate-limiting
- Bot protection (via Microsoft threat intelligence)

Use Cases:

- Protect APIs and web apps from OWASP Top 10 vulnerabilities
- Terminate SSL at the edge
- Route based on path or host headers

Azure Bastion

Azure Bastion allows secure RDP/SSH access to VMs directly from the Azure Portal without exposing VMs to the public internet.

Benefits:

- Reduces attack surface
- Encrypted and managed access
- No need for managing jumpboxes or IP allow lists

Use Cases:

- Managing production VMs securely
- Administering VMs from untrusted networks
- Compliance-focused environments

Private Link and Service Endpoints

Azure offers two powerful mechanisms for securing PaaS service traffic:

Service Endpoints:

- Extend VNet identity to Azure services (e.g., Azure SQL, Storage)
- Traffic remains within Azure backbone
- Simple configuration

Private Link:

- Access Azure services via a private IP address
- Prevents data exposure to public internet
- Supports custom DNS configuration

```
# Create a private endpoint for Blob Storage

az network private-endpoint create \

—name MyPrivateEndpoint \

—resource-group MyRG \
```

—vnet-name AppVNet \

—subnet MySubnet \

—private-connection-resource-id /subscriptions/.../Microsoft.Storage/storageAccounts/mystorage \

—group-id blob

Use Cases:

- Financial services requiring full network isolation
- Healthcare workloads subject to HIPAA compliance
- Enterprise policies forbidding outbound internet access

VPN Gateway and ExpressRoute

These services enable secure, encrypted communication between Azure and on-premises environments.

VPN Gateway:

- IPsec/IKE-based tunnel over the internet
- Site-to-site and point-to-site modes
- Active-active and BGP support

ExpressRoute:

- Private, dedicated link to Azure
- Higher throughput and SLA
- Can peer with Microsoft services directly (e.g., Microsoft 365)

Use Cases:

- Hybrid cloud environments
- Disaster recovery data replication
- Sensitive or regulated data scenarios

Security Monitoring and Policy

Azure Monitor and Network Watcher:

- Flow logs for NSGs and traffic analysis
- Packet capture for troubleshooting
- Connection troubleshooting diagnostics

Azure Policy:

- Enforce rules like "Only use private endpoints for storage"
- Audit or deny deployments violating security rules

Azure Blueprint:

- Deploy repeatable, compliant environments
- Combine NSGs, Policies, RBAC, and resources

Example: Enforce all storage accounts to deny public access.

```
{
"policyRule": {
```

```
"if": {
"field": "Microsoft.Storage/storageAccounts/allowBlobPublicAccess",
"equals": true
},
"then": {
"effect": "deny"
}
}
}
```

Best Practices for Network Security

1. **Segment your networks**: Use subnets and NSGs to enforce micro-segmentation.
2. **Apply least privilege**: Deny all by default, then allow explicitly.
3. **Use WAF and DDoS Standard** for web applications exposed to the internet.
4. **Centralize outbound traffic**: Route through Azure Firewall for inspection and logging.
5. **Prefer Private Link** over public endpoints for sensitive data.
6. **Use application security groups** for logical rule management.
7. **Enable logging** via Network Watcher and route to Log Analytics or Sentinel.

8. **Audit regularly**: Use Secure Score and Policy compliance data to track configuration drift.

Summary

Azure offers a comprehensive and flexible set of network security and access control tools that enable organizations to build highly secure environments tailored to their operational, regulatory, and business needs.

Key Takeaways:

- Virtual Networks, NSGs, and ASGs form the foundation of access control.

- Azure Firewall, WAF, and Bastion add advanced network-level protections.

- Service Endpoints and Private Link eliminate the need for public internet exposure.

- VPN and ExpressRoute support secure hybrid connectivity.

- Monitoring and governance tools enforce compliance and provide visibility.

With these capabilities, Azure enables enterprises to meet even the most stringent network security requirements in a scalable and maintainable way. The next section will cover identity services—another critical layer in Azure's security framework.

Azure Identity Services

Azure Identity Services provide a comprehensive suite of capabilities for managing authentication, authorization, user and application identities, and secure access across Azure and connected applications. At the heart of Azure Identity is Azure Active Directory (Azure AD), Microsoft's cloud-native identity and access management (IAM) service. Beyond the core directory, Azure offers a range of features—such as managed identities, Azure AD B2B and B2C, conditional access, multi-factor authentication, and identity protection—that together enable secure, seamless, and scalable identity solutions.

Azure Active Directory

Azure AD is a multi-tenant, cloud-based directory and identity management service. It supports:

- **User Management**: Create, update, and delete user objects; synchronize with on-premises AD using Azure AD Connect.
- **Group Management**: Organize users into groups for easier access control, licensing, and policy application.
- **Role-Based Access Control (RBAC)**: Grant permissions to Azure resources by assigning built-in or custom roles to users, groups, or service principals.
- **Application Registrations**: Configure single-sign-on (SSO) for custom and gallery applications via OAuth 2.0, OpenID Connect, SAML, and WS-Fed.
- **Federation**: Integrate external identity providers (e.g., ADFS, Google, Facebook) for seamless SSO.

```
# Create an Azure AD user

az ad user create \

—display-name "Jane Doe" \
```

```
—user-principal-name jane.doe@contoso.onmicrosoft.com \
—password "P@ssw0rd!" \
—force-change-password-next-login true
# Assign Reader role at subscription scope
az role assignment create \
—assignee jane.doe@contoso.onmicrosoft.com \
—role Reader \
—scope /subscriptions/{subscription-id}
```

Authentication Methods

Azure AD supports multiple authentication methods to balance security and user experience:

- **Password Hash Synchronization (PHS)**: Syncs on-premises passwords to Azure AD.
- **Pass-Through Authentication (PTA)**: Validates passwords directly against on-premises AD.
- **Federated Authentication**: Redirects authentication to an external Identity Provider (IdP) such as ADFS.
- **Passwordless Authentication**: Enables FIDO2 security keys, Microsoft Authenticator app push, and Windows Hello for Business.
- **Certificate-Based Authentication (CBA)**: Uses client certificates for strong user authentication.

Multi-Factor Authentication (MFA)

MFA adds an extra layer of security by requiring two or more verification methods:

- **Something you know**: Password or PIN.
- **Something you have**: Authenticator app, phone call, SMS, or hardware token.
- **Something you are**: Biometric (fingerprint or facial recognition).

Enable MFA registration policy

az ad msapolicy authenticationmethods policy update \

—id "RegistrationPolicy" \

—enabled-methods "MicrosoftAuthenticator, Fido2"

Feature highlights:

- **Per-user MFA**: Toggle MFA on individual accounts.
- **Conditional Access MFA**: Enforce MFA based on risk or location.
- **Verification options**: Authenticator push, TOTP codes, SMS, and voice.

Conditional Access

Conditional Access policies evaluate signals—user, device, location, application, and risk—to enforce automated access controls.

Key controls:

- **Require MFA** when accessing high-risk applications or from untrusted locations.
- **Block or grant access** based on user risk level (via Azure AD Identity Protection).
- **Require compliant or hybrid-joined devices.**
- **Session controls**: Enforce sign-in frequency or application restrictions.

```
# Example policy: require MFA for external access

az ad conditionalaccess policy create \

—display-name "Require MFA for External" \

—state enabled \

—conditions '{"users": {"include": ["All"]}, "locations": {"exclude": ["Trusted"]}}' \

—grant-controls '{"operator": "OR", "builtInControls": ["mfa"]}'
```

Managed Identities

Managed Identities eliminate the need for storing credentials in code or configuration:

- **System-Assigned Managed Identity**: Tied to a single Azure service instance; lifecycle matches the resource.
- **User-Assigned Managed Identity**: Independent Azure resource; can be shared across multiple services.

Use cases:

- Securely authenticate Azure Functions to Key Vault.

- Grant VMs access to Azure SQL without secrets.
- Connect App Service to Storage accounts safely.

```
# Enable system-assigned managed identity on a VM
az vm identity assign \
—resource-group MyRG \
—name MyVM
```

Azure AD B2B and B2C

Azure AD B2B (Business-to-Business):

- Enables collaboration by inviting external users to your Azure AD.
- External users use their own identities to access your resources.
- Simplifies governance with invitation workflows and access reviews.

Azure AD B2C (Business-to-Consumer):

- Provides customer-facing identity management.
- Supports social identity providers (Google, Facebook, LinkedIn), local accounts, and custom policies.
- Enables custom branding, user journeys, and seamless authentication.

```
# Create a B2C tenant link (via portal or PowerShell, CLI limited)
```

Azure AD Identity Protection

Identity Protection detects and remediates identity risks using adaptive machine learning:

• **Risk Events**: Impossible travel, leaked credentials, anonymous IP threat.

• **Risk Policies**: Block or require password change/MFA based on user or sign-in risk levels.

• **Reporting and Alerts**: Investigate risk events and user vulnerabilities.

Integration with On-Premises

Azure AD Connect synchronizes identity data and enables federation:

• **Directory synchronization**: Users, groups, and attributes.

• **Hybrid identity**: Single user account across on-prem and cloud.

• **Pass-through authentication** and **Federation** for seamless sign-on.

Azure AD Connect setup is performed via the installation wizard on a domain-joined server.

Identity Governance

Azure AD Identity Governance features help manage identity lifecycle and compliance:

• **Access Reviews**: Periodically review and certify user access.

- **Privileged Identity Management (PIM)**: Just-in-time elevation for privileged roles.
- **Entitlement Management**: Automated access packages and lifecycle.

```
# Activate PIM for role (via portal)
```

Best Practices

1. **Enforce MFA for all users**, especially privileged accounts.
2. **Implement Conditional Access** to adapt to risk signals.
3. **Use Managed Identities** over service principals where possible.
4. **Monitor sign-in logs** and set alerts for suspicious activities.
5. **Perform access reviews** quarterly to remove stale permissions.
6. **Secure on-premises integration** with least-privilege service accounts.
7. **Adopt passwordless options** to reduce phishing risk.

Summary

Azure Identity Services—including Azure AD, managed identities, B2B/B2C, conditional access, MFA, and identity protection—form a robust platform for securing identities and managing secure access across cloud and hybrid environments. These capabilities ensure that only authorized users and applications can access resources, and that identity risks are detected and mitigated in real time. Mastery of these services is critical for designing secure Azure solutions and for success in the AZ-900 certification.

Privacy and Compliance Resources

In the modern digital landscape, data privacy and regulatory compliance have become cornerstones of trust between technology providers and consumers. Microsoft Azure has established a comprehensive and transparent framework to help organizations meet global and industry-specific privacy requirements, manage data responsibly, and maintain regulatory compliance. Azure's approach is built upon five key pillars: transparency, control, security, compliance, and support.

This section covers Azure's privacy principles, built-in compliance resources, customer responsibilities, regulatory alignment, and how organizations can demonstrate and manage compliance within their Azure environments.

Microsoft's Commitment to Privacy

Microsoft positions itself not only as a technology provider but as a steward of customer data. Azure's privacy commitments include:

- **You own your data**: Microsoft does not use customer data for advertising or commercial purposes unrelated to service delivery.

- **You control your data**: Tools are available to access, export, and delete data on demand.

- **Data is protected**: Encryption at rest and in transit is default, with options for customer-managed keys.

- **Data location transparency**: Customers can choose the region where their data is stored and processed.

- **Data access**: Microsoft limits access to customer data, requiring justified need and extensive auditing.

These principles align with global privacy regulations such as GDPR (EU), CCPA (California), LGPD (Brazil), and others.

Azure Trust Center

The **Microsoft Trust Center** (https://www.microsoft.com/en-us/trust-center) is a publicly accessible portal that details Microsoft's approach to security, privacy, compliance, and transparency.

Key Sections:

- **Data Protection**: Information on encryption, secure development lifecycle, and incident response.
- **Compliance Offerings**: Lists certifications and attestations such as ISO 27001, SOC, FedRAMP, HIPAA, PCI-DSS, etc.
- **Regional Regulations**: Specific guidance for GDPR, UK Data Protection Act, etc.
- **Privacy Resources**: Whitepapers, audit reports, and data protection addendums.

This portal is essential for both IT leaders and compliance officers needing assurance and documentation on Azure's privacy practices.

Compliance Manager

Microsoft Compliance Manager is a dedicated solution in the Microsoft Purview (formerly Microsoft Compliance Center) suite that helps you manage your compliance posture within Azure and Microsoft 365.

Features:

- **Prebuilt assessments** for over 320 regulations (e.g., GDPR, NIST, ISO, HIPAA).
- **Real-time scoring** to assess compliance progress.
- **Actionable insights**: Prioritized improvement actions.
- **Workflow automation**: Assign tasks, track remediation, and document evidence.

Compliance Manager is accessed via Microsoft Purview portal; no CLI interface.

Use Case Example: An enterprise pursuing ISO 27001 certification can use Compliance Manager to track technical and procedural controls across Azure workloads, ensuring each clause is covered and documented.

Azure Blueprints for Compliance

Azure Blueprints enable you to deploy a governed environment that includes compliance-aligned resources, policies, and controls out-of-the-box.

Examples:

- **FedRAMP Blueprint**: Deploys baseline infrastructure and policies aligned with U.S. federal requirements.
- **ISO 27001 Blueprint**: Enforces security and auditing controls across deployed resources.

- **NIST SP 800-53 Blueprint**: Implements government-approved control sets.

Blueprints may include:

- Role-based access control (RBAC)
- Resource locks
- Azure Policy definitions
- Templates for secure resources

Assign a blueprint to a subscription (via portal or REST API)

Blueprints ensure consistent deployment of compliant environments across large-scale environments, especially important for highly regulated industries such as finance, healthcare, and government.

Azure Policy and Governance

Azure Policy helps enforce rules and effects over resources, ensuring they are compliant with your organization's or regulatory standards.

Features:

- **Deny or audit actions**: Prevent non-compliant deployments.
- **Initiatives**: Group related policies (e.g., "HIPAA Readiness" initiative).
- **Exemptions and remediation**: Temporary exemptions for resources, automated correction.
- **Integration with Compliance Manager** and Defender for Cloud.

{

```
"policyRule": {
"if": {
"field": "location",
"notEquals": "UK South"
},
"then": {
"effect": "deny"
}
}
}
```

Use Cases:

- Restrict deployments to specific geographic regions for data residency compliance.
- Require that storage accounts use customer-managed keys.
- Deny creation of public-facing virtual machines or databases.

Data Residency and Sovereignty

Azure enables customers to choose the region where data is stored and processed. Azure's **data residency model** ensures that:

- **Primary data storage remains within the selected region.**
- **Backups and replication follow rules aligned with local regulations.**

• **Geo-redundant services** may be optional or limited depending on sensitivity and compliance needs.

Data Sovereignty Support:

• **Azure Government Cloud**: Compliant with FedRAMP High, operated by U.S. citizens.

• **Azure China 21Vianet**: A physically and logically separated instance of Azure to meet Chinese regulations.

• **EU Data Boundary for Microsoft Cloud**: New initiative to ensure EU customer data remains and is processed within the EU.

Privacy by Design and Security Development Lifecycle

Azure services are built using Microsoft's **Security Development Lifecycle (SDL)** and **Privacy by Design** principles.

SDL Includes:

• Threat modeling

• Secure coding practices

• Automated code scanning

• Manual penetration testing

• Vulnerability response protocols

Privacy Engineering focuses on:

• Data minimization

• Purpose limitation

- Transparency controls
- Consent management and revocation

These foundational elements ensure that Azure services are designed with compliance and privacy as first-class citizens.

Auditing and Reporting

Azure enables extensive auditing, logging, and alerting capabilities, crucial for compliance and incident response.

Tools:

- **Azure Activity Logs**: Tracks all control-plane actions across resources.
- **Azure Resource Logs**: Captures data-plane operations.
- **Azure Monitor and Log Analytics**: Analyze, correlate, and visualize logs.
- **Microsoft Sentinel**: SIEM for real-time alerting and automated responses.
- **Microsoft Purview Audit**: Unified audit logs for data activities across Microsoft services.

Reporting Capabilities:

- Downloadable audit reports from the Trust Center.
- Role-specific dashboards in Compliance Manager.
- Built-in integrations with GRC (Governance, Risk, and Compliance) tools.

Customer Responsibilities

Azure operates on a **shared responsibility model** for compliance:

Layer	Microsoft	Customer
Physical Security	◈	◈
Infrastructure Security	◈	◈
OS-level Patching	Depends	◈ (IaaS), ◈ (PaaS)
Application Logic	◈	◈
Access Control	◈	◈
Data Classification & Handling	◈	◈

It is the customer's duty to:

- Classify and label sensitive data.
- Configure access controls and authentication policies.
- Apply encryption, backup, and monitoring policies.
- Maintain compliance documentation and review findings.

International and Industry-Specific Compliance

Azure supports over 100 compliance certifications and attestations across global jurisdictions and industry domains.

Global Examples:

- **ISO 27001, ISO 27018**
- **SOC 1, SOC 2, SOC 3**
- **CSA STAR, NIST, GDPR**

Industry-Specific Examples:

- **HIPAA/HITRUST** – Healthcare
- **PCI-DSS** – Payment processing
- **FedRAMP, CJIS, ITAR** – Government and defense
- **FISC, BAFIN, MAS** – Financial services

Azure's compliance offerings are verified by third-party auditors and are updated regularly as new standards emerge.

Summary

Azure's privacy and compliance resources empower organizations to build and maintain cloud environments that are secure, transparent, and aligned with regulatory and ethical obligations. Microsoft provides extensive tools, documentation, and certifications to support a compliant-by-default approach.

Key Takeaways:

- Azure is built with privacy and compliance at its core, following global frameworks.
- The Trust Center, Compliance Manager, and Blueprints offer visibility and control.
- Azure Policy and Purview provide enforcement and auditing mechanisms.
- Customers retain responsibility for configuring and operating compliant workloads.

- Azure's breadth of compliance certifications simplifies regulatory approval processes.

Understanding and leveraging these resources is essential for cloud architects, compliance officers, and developers seeking to build trusted, enterprise-grade solutions on Azure. In the next chapter, we'll turn to Azure pricing models, cost management tools, and service-level agreements to help you plan financially sustainable cloud deployments.

Chapter 5: Azure Pricing, SLA, and Lifecycle

Azure Subscriptions and Management Groups

Azure provides a scalable and flexible structure for organizing and managing access to resources through subscriptions and management groups. These elements form the administrative and billing hierarchy of the Azure platform. Understanding how they work is essential for effective governance, cost control, policy enforcement, and access management across enterprise or multi-project environments.

This section explores the purpose, structure, capabilities, and best practices for using Azure subscriptions, management groups, tenants, and related organizational constructs to establish scalable, secure, and cost-effective governance in the cloud.

Azure Tenants

An **Azure AD tenant** is a dedicated and trusted instance of Azure Active Directory, automatically created when your organization signs up for a Microsoft cloud service like Azure, Microsoft 365, or Dynamics 365.

Key Points:

- A tenant is tied to a single organization and represents its identity backbone.
- Each tenant is associated with one or more Azure subscriptions.

- Tenant ID is globally unique and controls directory-based services like user authentication, group management, and role assignment.

Use Cases:

- Centralized identity management
- Delegating access across multiple subscriptions
- Federation with on-prem Active Directory

Azure Subscriptions

An **Azure subscription** is a logical container used to provision resources in Azure. It holds the billing account for the services and resources created under it.

Key Characteristics:

- All resources are billed to the subscription.
- Subscriptions belong to an Azure AD tenant.
- A single tenant can contain multiple subscriptions.

Types of Subscriptions:

- **Pay-As-You-Go**: Billed monthly based on usage.
- **Enterprise Agreement (EA)**: Consolidated billing for large organizations.
- **Microsoft Customer Agreement (MCA)**: Modern alternative to EA.
- **Free Trial**: $200 credit for 30 days to explore services.

- **Azure for Students**: $100 in free credits without requiring a credit card.

View current subscriptions

az account list—output table

Use Cases:

- Separating billing and access control by department or environment (e.g., dev, test, prod)
- Implementing cost governance boundaries
- Managing quota limits for large-scale resource deployments

Subscription Management and Access Control

Azure uses **Role-Based Access Control (RBAC)** to manage permissions at the subscription level. Key roles include:

- **Owner**: Full access to manage resources, including access control.
- **Contributor**: Can manage resources but not permissions.
- **Reader**: View-only access to resources.
- **Billing Reader**: Access to view costs and billing info.

RBAC roles can be assigned at multiple scopes:

- Management group
- Subscription
- Resource group
- Individual resource

Best Practices:

- Assign roles to groups instead of individuals.
- Use **least privilege** principle—only grant the minimum required access.
- Regularly audit access assignments.

Management Groups

Management groups provide a hierarchy for organizing subscriptions at scale. They allow for the application of policies, RBAC roles, and compliance standards across multiple subscriptions efficiently.

Key Features:

- Support up to six levels of hierarchy (excluding root).
- Every subscription must belong to one management group.
- Policies and access control applied at the management group automatically propagate to all child subscriptions.

Example Hierarchy:

```
Tenant Root Group
├── Corp
│   ├── Finance
│   └── HR
├── DevOps
```

```
│ ├── Dev
│ └── QA
└── Production
```

```
# Create a management group (requires directory access)

az account management-group create—name CorpGroup—display-name "Corporate Group"
```

Use Cases:

- Apply organization-wide policies (e.g., allowed regions, tagging standards)
- Structure billing and resource alignment to departments
- Establish delegated administration per business unit

Resource Groups

Within a subscription, resources are organized into **resource groups**. These act as logical containers for related resources.

Characteristics:

- Resource groups provide scoping for lifecycle management.
- Deleting a resource group deletes all resources within it.
- Resources in a group can reside in different regions.

```
# Create a resource group

az group create—name AppRG—location westeurope
```

Use Cases:

- Grouping resources for an application (VMs, databases, storage)
- Applying RBAC and policies at the group level
- Supporting CI/CD and automation workflows

Azure Policy and Governance at Scale

Azure Policy can be applied at management group, subscription, or resource group levels to enforce rules and effects on resources.

Examples of Common Policies:

- Only allow deployment to certain regions.
- Require specific tags on all resources.
- Enforce encryption on storage accounts.

Azure Blueprints can also be deployed across subscriptions under a management group to standardize environment setup.

Subscription Quotas and Limits

Azure imposes quotas at the subscription level for resource types like:

- Virtual machines (per region)
- Storage accounts
- Public IP addresses
- vCPU limits

These quotas help prevent resource abuse and over-provisioning. Quotas can often be increased by submitting a request through the Azure portal.

Subscription Billing and Invoicing

Azure subscriptions track resource consumption for billing. The primary billing account is tied to the subscription.

Features:

- Billing data accessible via Cost Management + Billing.
- Invoices generated monthly.
- Azure Price Sheet and Rate Card APIs allow programmatic cost analysis.
- Tagging resources supports chargeback and showback reporting.

Key Concepts:

- **Billing Scope**: Defines what level (account, subscription) the invoice is created for.
- **Departments & Accounts (EA)**: Used to organize billing for large enterprises.
- **Billing Profiles (MCA)**: Track and manage invoices in consolidated views.

Subscription Lifecycle

Each Azure subscription follows a lifecycle:

1. **Creation** – New subscription provisioned (manual or automated).
2. **Active** – Fully operational, access and billing enabled.
3. **Disabled** – Payment overdue or expired; resources retained but inaccessible.
4. **Deprovisioned** – After a retention period, all data and resources are deleted.

Notifications:

- Azure sends email alerts for usage thresholds, renewals, and billing issues.

Cancellation and Deletion:

- Subscriptions can be canceled by the account admin.
- Deleted subscriptions cannot be recovered after the retention window.

Best Practices for Subscription and Management Structure

1. **Use management groups** for organizational alignment and governance.
2. **Segment workloads** across subscriptions by department, environment, or project.
3. **Apply RBAC roles** at the appropriate scope and minimize use of Owner.
4. **Use policies** to enforce compliance automatically.
5. **Implement tagging standards** across all subscriptions for cost tracking.
6. **Monitor usage and costs** with built-in cost management

tools.

7. **Use resource groups** to logically group related resources and manage them collectively.
8. **Document subscription purpose** in metadata or tags to reduce confusion at scale.
9. **Regularly audit access**, policies, and limits across all subscriptions.
10. **Use automation (ARM/Bicep/Terraform)** to create and configure subscriptions programmatically for large enterprises.

Summary

Azure subscriptions and management groups provide the administrative and financial backbone of an Azure deployment. They allow for isolation, access control, policy enforcement, and cost tracking across a multi-team, multi-project, or multi-region enterprise.

Key Takeaways:

- Subscriptions are billing units tied to an Azure AD tenant.

- Management groups organize subscriptions and support governance at scale.

- RBAC and Azure Policy allow for granular control and standardization.

- Resource groups help manage and logically group related services.

- Using these constructs effectively enables scalable and compliant Azure adoption.

In the next section, we'll explore the cost management tools and pricing calculators Azure offers to help you optimize spending, estimate future costs, and control cloud budgets.

Cost Management Tools and Calculators

Effective cost management is essential to a successful and sustainable cloud strategy. Microsoft Azure offers a comprehensive suite of tools to help users estimate, monitor, optimize, and govern cloud spending. These tools support a wide range of financial management practices, from initial budgeting and forecasting to real-time cost tracking and optimization across teams and departments.

This section covers Azure's cost estimation, management, and optimization features. It also includes strategies for implementing financial accountability in the cloud through governance policies, alerts, tagging, and reporting.

Azure Pricing Calculator

The **Azure Pricing Calculator** (https://azure.microsoft.com/en-us/pricing/calculator/) allows users to estimate the cost of Azure services before deployment. It helps in planning cloud solutions by simulating various configurations, scaling options, and deployment regions.

Key Features:

- Add and configure multiple Azure services in a single view
- Customize instance sizes, storage tiers, and region-specific pricing
- Export cost estimates as Excel files or shareable links

- Visualize monthly vs. upfront costs

Use Cases:

- Pre-sales planning for clients or internal stakeholders
- Comparing different architectures for cost impact
- Estimating operational expenses before a cloud migration

Best Practice: Always include expected usage levels (compute hours, storage size, data transfer) and reserve instance options when building estimates.

Azure Total Cost of Ownership (TCO) Calculator

The **Azure TCO Calculator** compares the cost of running workloads in an on-premises environment versus migrating to Azure.

Input Parameters:

- Server workloads (quantity, type, CPU/memory usage)
- Storage and networking needs
- Software licensing costs
- IT labor and datacenter operational costs

Output:

- Detailed 3-year or 5-year cost projection
- Capital expenditure (CapEx) vs. operational expenditure (OpEx)
- Total cost savings from Azure migration

Use Cases:

- Building business cases for executive approval
- Highlighting long-term ROI of cloud adoption
- Justifying migration from legacy systems

Azure Cost Management + Billing

Azure Cost Management + Billing is a native tool in the Azure Portal that enables tracking, analyzing, and optimizing Azure spend across subscriptions and billing scopes.

Key Components:

- **Cost Analysis**: Visualizes spend by resource, resource group, service, location, or tags.
- **Budgets**: Set and monitor spending limits.
- **Alerts**: Notify stakeholders when budgets approach thresholds.
- **Forecasts**: Predict future spending trends based on historical usage.
- **Exports**: Schedule recurring cost data exports to storage accounts.
- **Marketplace Charges**: Analyze usage of third-party resources from the Azure Marketplace.

```
# Example: Schedule cost export using Azure CLI

az costmanagement export create \

—name "DailyCostExport" \
```

```
—timeframe MonthToDate \

—dataset-configuration grain=Daily \

—export-type ActualCost \

—storage-account-id
"/subscriptions/<subId>/resourceGroups/<rg>/providers/
Microsoft.Storage/storageAccounts/<account>"
```

Azure Budgets and Alerts

Budgets allow you to define spending thresholds for subscriptions, resource groups, or specific services. Alerts notify users when spend approaches or exceeds defined limits.

Budget Configuration Options:

- Time period: Monthly, quarterly, annually
- Scope: Subscription, resource group, or management group
- Alert thresholds: % of budget (e.g., 80%, 100%, 120%)
- Actions: Email notifications or automated workflows via Action Groups

Use Cases:

- Prevent cost overruns in sandbox or dev environments
- Alert finance teams before billing anomalies
- Control costs on pay-as-you-go plans

Cost Allocation with Tags

Resource tagging enables fine-grained cost attribution across teams, departments, or projects.

Best Practices:

- Standardize tags (e.g., Environment, Project, CostCenter, Owner)
- Use **Azure Policy** to enforce mandatory tagging during resource creation
- Monitor tag coverage using **Azure Resource Graph**

Example Tags:

```
{
"Environment": "Production",
"Department": "Finance",
"Project": "ForecastingAPI",
"Owner": "jane.doe@company.com"
}
```

Use Cases:

- Chargeback and showback models in enterprise IT
- Cross-team accountability for resource usage
- Identifying unused or orphaned resources

Reservation Recommendations and Savings Plans

Azure offers **cost-saving options** for predictable workloads:

Azure Reserved Instances (RIs):

- Commit to 1- or 3-year terms for specific VM series or databases
- Up to 72% discount vs. pay-as-you-go pricing
- Scope to single subscription or shared across billing scopes

Azure Savings Plans:

- Flexible alternative to RIs with commitment to a fixed hourly spend
- Covers a wide range of services: VMs, App Service, Functions, etc.
- Provides flexibility to switch regions, series, and OS

Best Practices:

- Use **Azure Advisor** for personalized reservation recommendations
- Evaluate workloads with stable usage patterns before purchasing reservations

---

Azure Advisor

Azure Advisor is a personalized recommendation engine that analyzes your configurations and usage to provide cost-saving and performance-improving suggestions.

Recommendation Categories:

- Cost: Identify underutilized VMs, over-provisioned resources
- Security: Secure open endpoints and misconfigured firewalls
- High Availability: Configure backup, autoscale, zone redundancy
- Operational Excellence: Optimize governance and automation

Use Cases:

- Reduce idle resource spend
- Optimize compute sizing based on CPU/memory usage
- Adopt reservation opportunities

Programmatic Cost Management

Azure provides APIs and SDKs to query and export cost data for integration into custom dashboards, enterprise billing systems, or third-party financial tools.

REST APIs:

- **Usage Details API**: Resource-level usage records
- **Forecast API**: Budget projection and anomaly detection
- **Budget API**: Manage budget objects via code

SDKs:

- Azure SDKs for .NET, Python, Java, Node.js

```
# Retrieve forecasted cost

az costmanagement forecast show \

—timeframe MonthToDate \

—scope "/subscriptions/<subscription-id>"
```

Use Cases:

- Embed cost analysis in ITSM or ERP platforms
- Build cost dashboards with Power BI
- Trigger cost-based governance actions via Logic Apps

Multi-Cloud and Cross-Tenant Billing

For enterprises with hybrid or multi-cloud strategies, Azure Cost Management supports integration with:

- **AWS billing data** via connector
- **Microsoft Customer Agreement** (**MCA**) billing scopes
- **Consolidated billing reports** across tenants with cross-directory access

Benefits:

- Centralized cloud financial management
- Unified reporting for cross-cloud usage
- Improved visibility for enterprise finance teams

Cost Optimization Strategies

1. **Rightsize VMs** using Azure Advisor's usage insights.
2. **Use spot VMs** for stateless workloads (up to 90% discount).
3. **Shut down dev/test environments** during non-working hours.
4. **Implement autoscaling** for web apps and services.
5. **Use storage lifecycle rules** to move data to cheaper tiers.
6. **Clean up unused public IPs, disks, and NICs.**
7. **Tag resources and enforce tagging policies.**
8. **Regularly review budget thresholds and export billing data.**

Summary

Azure offers robust and integrated tools to estimate, monitor, control, and optimize cloud costs. These tools are essential for ensuring that organizations can scale efficiently without compromising financial oversight or governance.

Key Takeaways:

- The Pricing Calculator and TCO tools help with initial planning and business case development.
- Azure Cost Management + Billing provides ongoing spend analysis, alerting, and forecasting.
- Budgets, tags, policies, and reservations enable proactive cost control.
- Azure Advisor and automation tools simplify cost-saving operations.

- Programmatic access to cost data supports integration into enterprise systems and reporting dashboards.

Mastering these tools empowers IT teams, developers, and financial stakeholders to work collaboratively toward sustainable and cost-effective cloud adoption. In the next section, we'll explore how Azure's SLAs provide availability guarantees and what they mean for service design and operational planning.

Service Level Agreements (SLAs)

Service Level Agreements (SLAs) are foundational to understanding the reliability and availability commitments made by Microsoft Azure for its cloud services. An SLA defines the guaranteed level of service performance, usually expressed as a percentage of uptime over a given period, and outlines the compensation customers can receive if Azure fails to meet these guarantees. These guarantees help organizations plan their architectures, define business continuity strategies, and assess the risk of downtime.

This section provides an in-depth exploration of Azure SLAs, including their structure, examples across services, calculation methods, architectural considerations, financial implications, and practical guidance for integrating SLAs into operational and design strategies.

Understanding SLAs in Azure

An SLA in Azure is a formal document that describes:

- The service scope covered by the agreement
- The guaranteed availability or performance metric
- The conditions under which the guarantee applies

- The compensation (typically in service credits) if Azure fails to meet the commitment

Azure typically defines availability as the percentage of time a service is accessible and functioning as expected, excluding planned maintenance or user-triggered downtime.

Example Format:

SLA Metric	**Value**
Monthly Uptime	99.9%
Permitted Downtime	~43.8 minutes/month
Compensation Threshold	Below 99.9%

Common Availability SLAs by Service

Azure offers SLAs across its core services. These vary by configuration, redundancy, and service tier.

Virtual Machines (VMs)

- **Single VM with Premium SSDs in an Availability Set**: 99.9%
- **Two or more VMs in an Availability Set or Zone**: 99.95%
- **VMs across Availability Zones**: 99.99%

Azure App Service

- **Standard or Premium Plan**: 99.95%
- **Free/Shared Plans**: No SLA

Azure SQL Database

- **Single Database or Elastic Pool**: 99.99%
- **Managed Instance**: 99.99%

Azure Storage

- **Read-access geo-redundant storage (RA-GRS)**: 99.99% for read access
- **Locally-redundant storage (LRS)**: 99.9%

Azure Kubernetes Service (AKS)

- **API server availability**: 99.95% when using Availability Zones

Azure DNS

- **DNS query availability**: 100%

Refer to the official SLA documentation athttps://azure.microsoft.com/en-us/support/legal/sla/ for the latest and most complete information.

SLA Calculation and Composite Availability

SLAs apply per service, but in real-world applications, multiple services are typically combined. To estimate the overall availability of a solution, you must multiply the individual availabilities—a concept known as **composite SLA**.

Example:

Assume an app uses the following services:

- Azure App Service: 99.95%
- Azure SQL Database: 99.99%

Composite SLA = 0.9995 × 0.9999 ≈ 0.9994 = **99.94%**

This means your end-to-end solution can be expected to be available ~99.94% of the time, or about 26.3 minutes of downtime per month.

SLA Tiers and Service Design Implications

Availability SLAs often vary depending on the service configuration or pricing tier. Selecting higher tiers may provide better availability and tighter SLA guarantees.

Considerations:

- **Redundancy matters**: Many higher SLAs require the use of Availability Sets or Zones.
- **Storage class impacts**: Premium storage and geo-redundant options typically offer better guarantees.
- **Networking and DNS**: Services like Traffic Manager and Azure Front Door can improve resiliency but come with their own SLAs.

Best Practices:

- Deploy across Availability Zones or regions where supported.

- Use load balancers and health probes to detect and route around failures.
- Monitor SLA compliance using tools like Azure Monitor and Log Analytics.

SLA Exclusions and Limitations

Azure SLAs include specific **conditions and exclusions**:

Common Exclusions:

- Downtime during scheduled maintenance
- Previews or beta services (non-GA)
- Issues caused by customer-side misconfigurations
- Internet outages or third-party service failures
- Situations beyond Microsoft's reasonable control (force majeure)

Each SLA document provides a detailed list of exclusions. Customers must design for failure and understand what constitutes SLA-covered downtime.

Service Credit Structure

When Microsoft fails to meet an SLA, affected customers are eligible for **service credits**, not refunds.

Typical Credit Model:

Monthly Uptime	Service Credit
< 99.9%	10%
< 99%	25%
< 95%	100%

To claim credits:

1. Submit a support ticket within 30 days of the outage.
2. Provide incident details and logs.
3. Wait for Microsoft's verification and credit application.

Note: Credits apply only to the impacted service and billing period. They are not cumulative or stackable.

Monitoring and Validating SLAs

To ensure SLA commitments are met, organizations should implement proactive monitoring:

Tools:

- **Azure Monitor**: Alerts, metrics, and dashboards
- **Log Analytics**: Query availability trends across services
- **Application Insights**: Detect performance degradations
- **Availability Tests**: Perform synthetic transactions

```
# Create a metric alert for VM uptime

az monitor metrics alert create \
```

—name "VMUptimeAlert" \

—resource-group MyRG \

—scopes "/subscriptions/<id>/resourceGroups/MyRG/providers/Microsoft.Compute/virtualMachines/MyVM" \

—condition "avg Percentage CPU > 90" \

—description "CPU usage exceeded threshold"

Recommendations:

- Enable diagnostic logs on all services.
- Create alert rules for availability events.
- Log all incidents and use them for SLA impact analysis.

SLAs for Preview and Experimental Services

Services in **Preview**, **Beta**, or **Private Preview** phases do not carry SLA guarantees. These services are intended for testing, evaluation, and feedback and should never be used in production workloads without risk mitigation strategies.

Best practice is to isolate such components or avoid them altogether in production environments until GA (General Availability) release.

Business Continuity and SLAs

SLAs help define and inform **Business Continuity Plans (BCP)** and **Disaster Recovery (DR)** strategies. However, they are **not a substitute** for proper resilience planning.

Key Planning Elements:

- **Recovery Time Objective (RTO)**: How fast you can recover.
- **Recovery Point Objective (RPO)**: Maximum data loss in time.
- **Failover Design**: Use region-pairing and geo-redundant services.
- **Test DR Scenarios**: Simulate outages to verify failover success.

Azure offers **paired regions** with data replication and service failover priority to support high availability architectures across geographies.

Legal and Operational Relevance of SLAs

SLAs are legally binding documents and part of your Azure agreement. Organizations should:

- Integrate SLAs into service contracts with internal/external stakeholders.
- Use SLAs to define incident thresholds and escalation policies.
- Align SLAs with corporate risk tolerance and compliance requirements.

Summary

SLAs are critical to understanding the reliability, resilience, and service expectations of Azure workloads. By leveraging and designing around these guarantees, organizations can reduce risk, maintain operational continuity, and hold Microsoft accountable when services fall short.

Key Takeaways:

- Azure provides service-specific SLAs that define uptime and performance guarantees.
- Composite SLAs reflect the true end-to-end availability of a solution.
- Higher tiers and redundancy configurations often provide higher SLAs.
- Service credits are issued upon request when guarantees are not met.
- Monitoring, logging, and availability testing are crucial for SLA validation.
- SLAs must be integrated into business continuity, risk management, and compliance strategies.

In the next section, we will explore the lifecycle of Azure services, from preview to general availability, deprecation, and retirement—and how organizations can manage change effectively across evolving cloud environments.

Lifecycle in Azure Services

Azure services follow a defined lifecycle that governs how features and products are introduced, supported, evolved, and retired. Understanding this lifecycle is essential for cloud architects, developers, and IT operations professionals to make informed decisions about technology adoption, risk mitigation, and long-term supportability. The Azure service lifecycle includes several key phases: preview, general availability, mainstream support, deprecation, and retirement.

This section explains each phase of the lifecycle in detail, along with practical guidance on how to manage transitions, maintain compliance, and architect for long-term resilience.

Overview of the Azure Service Lifecycle

The Azure service lifecycle defines the journey of a service or feature from its inception to its eventual retirement. This framework ensures that customers are informed and empowered at every stage of the product's evolution.

Common Lifecycle Phases:

1. **Private Preview**
2. **Public Preview**
3. **General Availability (GA)**
4. **Sustained Support**
5. **Deprecation Announcement**
6. **Retirement**

These stages apply to services (e.g., Azure Cosmos DB), features (e.g., Azure Functions Premium Plan), and APIs (e.g., REST versioning).

Private Preview

The **Private Preview** phase is the earliest form of release for a service or feature. It is available to a limited set of invited customers for closed testing and feedback.

Characteristics:

- Access is invite-only.

- No public documentation or official support.
- Frequent breaking changes and rearchitecture possible.
- Not covered by SLAs.
- Should never be used in production workloads.

Use Cases:

- Organizations partnering with Microsoft for early innovation.
- Validation of product-market fit for specific industries.
- Feedback and feature influence opportunities.

Best Practice: Test in isolated environments only. Avoid dependencies in live systems.

Public Preview

The **Public Preview** phase makes the service available to all Azure users for evaluation and testing purposes.

Characteristics:

- Public documentation is available.
- Some services may be region-locked or feature-limited.
- No SLA or production support guarantee.
- Pricing may be reduced or free during preview.
- Subject to change without notice.

```
# Example: Enabling preview feature in Azure CLI
```

az feature register—namespace "Microsoft.ContainerService"—name "EnablePodSecurityPolicyPreview"

Considerations:

- Use in test/dev environments to evaluate capabilities.
- Monitor product updates and announcements regularly.
- Be prepared for API changes or reconfiguration requirements.

General Availability (GA)

General Availability marks the full commercial release of a service, indicating that Microsoft considers the service stable, supported, and production-ready.

Characteristics:

- Covered by SLAs and full technical support.
- Governed by Microsoft's customer agreement and legal terms.
- Available across most or all Azure regions.
- Pricing and billing enter full enforcement.

Implications:

- Production use is supported and recommended.
- Integrations and automation can now assume stability.
- Compliance requirements (e.g., ISO, SOC, GDPR) are typically met.

Best Practice: Wait for GA status before rolling out a service in mission-critical workloads unless explicitly approved and architected for change.

Sustained Support and Evolution

After GA, Azure services enter a period of sustained support and iterative enhancement.

Key Events:

- Introduction of new SKUs or tiers.
- Deprecation of older API versions.
- Release of integrations with Azure Monitor, Policy, and ARM templates.
- Expansion to new regions and availability zones.

Management Recommendations:

- Track service roadmap updates via the **Azure Updates** feed.
- Use ARM/Bicep templates or Terraform for infrastructure automation.
- Regularly test failover, scalability, and backup strategies.
- Integrate service monitoring into operational runbooks.

Deprecation Announcement

Deprecation refers to the formal announcement that a service, feature, or API version will be retired in the future.

Characteristics:

- Microsoft provides advance notice, typically 12 months.
- Official announcement via Azure Updates or documentation.
- Customers are encouraged to migrate to successor services or versions.
- SLA continues until the retirement date.

Examples:

- Azure Cloud Services (classic) was deprecated in favor of Azure App Services.
- Azure Storage SDKs v2.x were deprecated in favor of v12.x.

Migration Planning:

- Identify dependencies using Azure Resource Graph or Policy.
- Validate compatibility with new versions in a staging environment.
- Engage Microsoft support or partners for architectural review.

Retirement

Retirement is the final stage where a service or feature is shut down and no longer accessible or supported.

Characteristics:

- Occurs after the deprecation timeline has passed.
- Services are disabled and may be deleted by Microsoft.

- No SLA, support, or data recovery is available post-retirement.
- Final reminders sent to subscription owners and administrators.

Operational Impact:

- Failure to migrate results in service outages.
- APIs return errors or fail to connect.
- Resources may be marked as non-compliant in governance tools.

Best Practice: Implement resource lifecycle tracking and alerting to avoid last-minute scrambles.

Versioning and API Lifecycle

Many Azure services (e.g., Azure REST APIs, ARM APIs, SDKs) follow a versioning model tied to lifecycle stages.

Version Statuses:

- **Preview Versions**: Not supported in production.
- **GA Versions**: Supported and stable.
- **Deprecated Versions**: Will be removed in future; usage should cease.

Strategies:

- Use explicit API versions in code and templates.
- Monitor deprecation notices via SDK and CLI changelogs.
- Avoid using "latest" as API version in production scripts.

Azure Update Resources

Stay informed of lifecycle changes using the following resources:

- **Azure Updates**:https://azure.microsoft.com/en-us/updates/
- **Azure Service Health**: Personalized alerts for your subscriptions.
- **Azure Advisor**: Highlights deprecated services in use.
- **Azure Resource Graph**: Identify services at scale with Kusto queries.

```
Resources
| where type =~ 'microsoft.compute/virtualmachines'
| project name, location, properties.hardwareProfile.vmSize
```

Governance and Lifecycle Policy

To manage lifecycle transitions effectively, organizations should implement internal **cloud governance policies**.

Recommendations:

1. **Maintain a service catalog**: Track all Azure services in use and their lifecycle state.
2. **Implement tagging standards**: Include tags like ServiceOwner, LifecycleStage, DeprecationDate.
3. **Set expiration alerts** for deprecated services.
4. **Use Azure Policy** to block deployment of preview or deprecated SKUs.
5. **Conduct quarterly cloud reviews** with stakeholders to assess lifecycle impacts.

Summary

The Azure service lifecycle framework ensures that customers have visibility into the support and stability of services they depend on. Awareness of each lifecycle phase allows organizations to innovate responsibly, plan transitions proactively, and avoid the risks associated with deprecated or retired technologies.

Key Takeaways:

- Azure services evolve through preview, general availability, support, deprecation, and retirement phases.

- Each phase has specific support levels, SLAs, and operational implications.

- Preview features should not be used in production unless explicitly reviewed.

- Deprecation announcements require prompt planning to avoid service disruption.

- Proactive governance and automation are essential to manage lifecycle risks at scale.

Understanding the lifecycle of Azure services is fundamental to building resilient, compliant, and future-ready cloud architectures. This concludes our exploration of Azure pricing, SLAs, and service lifecycle management. In the next chapter, we'll shift to hands-on labs that help reinforce your knowledge through practical Azure exercises.

Chapter 6: Hands-On Labs and Practice Scenarios

Setting Up a Free Azure Account

Setting up a free Microsoft Azure account is the first step toward gaining practical, hands-on experience with cloud computing. Whether you're preparing for the AZ-900 certification, exploring career opportunities in cloud technologies, or testing solutions for your organization, the free account provides a risk-free environment to learn and experiment with core Azure services.

In this section, we walk through the complete process of creating a free Azure account, explain the free tier benefits, review setup requirements, and explore key services you can access without incurring charges. We'll also discuss best practices to manage usage, avoid unnecessary costs, and prepare your environment for hands-on labs throughout this book.

Overview of the Azure Free Account

Microsoft Azure offers a **free account** that includes access to a limited selection of services and a credit to explore paid services.

Key Benefits:

- **$200 in credits** valid for the first 30 days.
- **12 months of free services** including VMs, storage, databases, and more.
- **Always-free services** with usage caps (e.g., Azure Functions, Event Grid).

Free Services for 12 Months (Examples):

Service	Free Limit
Windows/Linux VM	750 hours/month (B1S VM)
Azure Blob Storage	5 GB LRS storage
SQL Database	250 GB storage
Bandwidth	15 GB outbound data transfer

Always Free (As long as account is active):

Service	Free Limit
Azure Functions	1 million requests/month
Event Grid	100,000 operations/month
App Service	1 GB outbound data/month
Cosmos DB	1,000 RU/s with 25 GB storage

These offerings allow you to follow all the hands-on labs in this chapter without exceeding free-tier limits if resources are managed carefully.

Prerequisites for Setting Up

Before creating your Azure account, ensure you meet the following requirements:

- A **Microsoft account** (Outlook.com, Live.com, Hotmail.com, etc.)
- A **valid phone number** for identity verification
- A **credit card or debit card** (for identity verification only—no charges without explicit upgrades)
- An **email address** you can access for verification

Microsoft uses the card and phone number to prevent abuse of the free trial program but does not charge unless you opt into a paid subscription.

Step-by-Step: Creating the Free Azure Account

1. **Navigate to the Azure Free Account Page**

Go to:https://azure.microsoft.com/free

Click on **"Start free"** to begin the signup process.

1. **Sign In or Create Microsoft Account**

Log in with your Microsoft account. If you do not have one, create a new one using your preferred email address or a new Outlook account.

1. **Identity Verification**

Provide your:

- Country/region
- Name
- Phone number (a code will be sent for verification)

1. **Credit/Debit Card Verification**

Enter your card details. Azure will authorize a small amount (typically $1) to verify the card, which will be refunded.

1. **Review and Accept Agreement**

Read through and accept the Microsoft Azure agreement, privacy statement, and offer details.

1. **Activate and Access the Portal**

Once verification is complete, your account is active. You'll be redirected to the **Azure Portal** athttps://portal.azure.com[5] where you can start using services.

Navigating the Azure Portal

The **Azure Portal** is the web-based interface for managing Azure services. Key sections include:

- **Home**: Overview and quickstart tiles
- **All Services**: Browse or search all Azure offerings
- **Resource Groups**: Logical containers for grouping related resources
- **Marketplace**: Deploy third-party or Microsoft-provided solutions
- **Cost Management + Billing**: Track and analyze usage and costs
- **Dashboard**: Customize with charts, shortcuts, and status widgets

```
# Verify access via Azure CLI (optional)

az login
```

Once logged in, you can start using tools like Azure Cloud Shell and Azure CLI directly within the portal.

5. https://portal.azure.com/

Best Practices for Managing Your Free Trial

To make the most of your free account:

Monitor Usage

- Use **Cost Management + Billing** to set up alerts.
- Review the **Usage + quotas** blade in the portal regularly.
- Enable email notifications for budget thresholds.

Use Resource Groups

- Group related services (VM, storage, network) into **resource groups.**
- Deleting the resource group removes all associated services—reduces risk of forgotten resources incurring charges.

Tag Resources

- Use tags such as Environment=Trial, Project=AZ900, Owner=YourName for easier filtering and cleanup.

Set Auto-Shutdown

For virtual machines, enable **auto-shutdown** to avoid unnecessary usage.

```
# Set VM auto-shutdown to 7 PM UTC

az vm auto-shutdown \

—resource-group MyResourceGroup \
```

```
—name MyVM \
—time 1900 \
—time-zone "UTC"
```

Transitioning Beyond the Free Trial

After 30 days or once your $200 credit is used, Azure pauses all services unless you **explicitly upgrade** to a pay-as-you-go subscription.

Upgrade Process:

- Navigate to the **Subscriptions** section
- Click **Upgrade**
- You retain access to:
    - Always-free services
    - Previously created resources (subject to usage and payment)

Tips:

- Delete unused resources before upgrading.
- Review estimated monthly costs using the **Pricing Calculator**.
- Consider setting up **budgets** to control spend.

Using the Free Account for Certification Practice

With your Azure free account, you can complete all of the following common AZ-900 tasks:

- Deploy Linux and Windows virtual machines
- Create and manage resource groups
- Use storage accounts for Blob and File storage
- Launch simple web apps in App Service
- Explore databases (SQL, Cosmos DB, etc.)
- Practice with Azure Functions and Event Grid
- Use Azure Monitor to observe resource metrics
- Create dashboards and alerts

Each of these tasks will be covered in detail in the next few sections of this chapter.

Summary

Setting up a free Azure account is the gateway to hands-on cloud learning and real-world experimentation. With $200 in credits and access to over 55 services in the free tier, learners can gain direct experience with nearly every concept tested on the AZ-900 exam.

Key Takeaways:

- Azure offers a generous free trial to help new users learn and explore the platform.

- The setup process is quick, secure, and only requires basic identity verification.

- The Azure Portal is the central hub for deploying and managing cloud resources.
- Monitoring usage, tagging resources, and using resource groups will help control costs.
- Transitioning to a paid plan is optional and can be postponed until you're ready.

With your account ready, you can now begin deploying and configuring Azure resources. The next section will walk through the Azure Portal interface in detail and show how to navigate it effectively for exam preparation and practical tasks.

Navigating the Azure Portal

The Azure Portal is the central, web-based user interface for interacting with Microsoft Azure's services, resources, and administrative functions. It provides an intuitive dashboard, a customizable workspace, and a unified environment to create, manage, monitor, and delete resources in a secure, graphical manner. Whether you're a beginner preparing for the AZ-900 exam or a seasoned cloud administrator, understanding how to navigate the Azure Portal is essential for managing cloud infrastructure effectively.

This section explores the structure of the Azure Portal, explains each key component and panel, demonstrates common operations, introduces essential features like the Cloud Shell and Marketplace, and offers best practices for personalizing your experience and optimizing your productivity.

Accessing the Azure Portal

The Azure Portal can be accessed via any modern web browser at:

https://portal.azure.com[6]

Use your Microsoft account to sign in. This account must be associated with an active Azure subscription (such as the free trial).

Portal Layout and Core Components

Once signed in, you'll encounter the default **dashboard** interface, which contains several core UI components:

1. Global Search Bar

Located at the top of the portal, the search bar allows quick access to resources, services, documentation, and help. Start typing the name of a service (e.g., "Virtual Machine") to jump directly to that service's pane.

2. Navigation Sidebar (Left Menu)

Includes key links to:

- **Home**: Returns you to the dashboard
- **Dashboard**: View and customize tiles
- **All Services**: Browse all Azure offerings
- **Resource Groups**: Logical groupings of related resources
- **Subscriptions**: View billing and subscription details

6. https://portal.azure.com/

- **Cost Management + Billing**: Analyze costs and budgets
- **Help + Support**: Open or manage support requests

3. Command Bar

Includes icons for notifications (bell), Cloud Shell (terminal icon), settings, directory switching, and feedback.

4. Service Panes and Blades

Azure uses a "blade" model—clicking on a service or resource opens a new panel (blade) that slides out, providing contextual information and settings.

Searching and Pinning Services

You can find any Azure service by using the **"All Services"** option or the global search bar.

Steps to Find and Pin a Service:

1. Click **"All Services"**
2. Search for a service, e.g., "Storage accounts"
3. Click the **star icon** to pin it to your sidebar for quick access

This is useful for frequently used services like Virtual Machines, App Services, SQL Databases, and Storage.

Creating a New Resource

To deploy any service in Azure, click the **"+ Create a resource"** button in the upper-left corner or use the **Marketplace**.

Example: Deploying a Storage Account

1. Go to **Home** > **Create a resource** > **Storage** > **Storage account**
2. Choose the subscription and resource group
3. Enter a unique storage account name
4. Select region, performance, replication, and access tier
5. Review and click **Create**

Once the deployment completes, a blade will open with your resource's details.

Managing Resource Groups

Resource Groups are containers that hold related resources. They simplify management by grouping VMs, databases, networking components, and storage under a single name.

Tasks You Can Perform:

- Add or remove resources
- Apply tags for cost tracking
- View cost analysis by group
- Delete all resources in a group at once

```
# Create a resource group using Azure CLI

az group create—name WebAppGroup—location westeurope
```

Monitoring and Metrics

Every Azure resource includes built-in **Monitoring** options. Use the Monitoring pane of a resource to:

- View CPU/memory/network usage
- Configure alerts based on thresholds
- Access diagnostics logs
- Integrate with **Azure Monitor** or **Log Analytics**

You can also add these metrics to your dashboard as tiles for real-time visibility.

Customizing the Dashboard

The dashboard is the first screen you see upon logging in. It's fully customizable and can display charts, shortcuts, resource overviews, and more.

Customization Steps:

1. Click **"Dashboard"** > **Edit**
2. Use the toolbox on the left to drag tiles into place
3. Resize, rename, or remove tiles
4. Click **Done Customizing** to save

You can create **multiple dashboards** for different teams or projects and share them across your organization.

Azure Cloud Shell

Azure Cloud Shell is a browser-based shell built into the portal that allows you to use **Bash** or **PowerShell** to run Azure CLI or PowerShell commands without needing to install anything locally.

Features:

- Persistent storage (mounted to /home directory)
- Preinstalled tools (git, az CLI, kubectl)
- Integrated code editor (Visual Studio Code experience)

Example: List running virtual machines

az vm list—show-details—query "[?powerState=='VM running'].{Name:name, Location:location}"—output table

Launch it by clicking the terminal icon in the top toolbar or pressing Shift + (backtick).

Azure Marketplace

The **Azure Marketplace** provides preconfigured solutions and templates for deploying popular software, services, and configurations.

Categories include:

- Virtual machine images
- Web applications
- Kubernetes and container services
- Network appliances (e.g., firewalls, load balancers)

- Databases and data analytics stacks

Example Use Case: Deploy a preconfigured WordPress website on Azure App Service.

Settings and Directory Management

Under the **Settings (gear icon)**, you can:

- Change themes (light, dark, high contrast)
- Configure language and region
- Manage personal preferences

Use the **Directory + Subscription filter** (top-right corner) to switch between tenants or subscriptions—especially useful for consultants, MSPs, or developers using multiple environments.

Accessing Help and Documentation

You can find help at any time by clicking the **"?" icon** in the upper-right. It offers:

- Guided tours of common tasks
- Quickstart tutorials
- Microsoft Learn modules
- Direct links to product documentation
- The ability to open support tickets

Best Practices for Using the Azure Portal

1. **Pin frequently used services** to the sidebar for easy access.

2. **Name resources consistently** with environment, project, and type (e.g., prod-web-vm01).
3. **Use dashboards** to visualize real-time metrics and resource status.
4. **Configure role-based access control (RBAC)** via portal for team collaboration.
5. **Enable monitoring and diagnostics** on all critical services.
6. **Automate deployments** after testing them through the portal UI.
7. **Use Cloud Shell** for repeatable commands, quick CLI access, and script testing.
8. **Create templates from portal deployments** for Infrastructure as Code (IaC) strategies.

Summary

The Azure Portal is a powerful and user-friendly interface that provides complete control over your Azure environment. Mastering portal navigation enhances productivity, reduces errors, and lays the groundwork for more advanced tasks like automation, scripting, and cost management.

Key Takeaways:

- Use the portal's sidebar, dashboard, and search features for efficient navigation.

- Create, monitor, and delete resources using blades and service-specific menus.

- Group related services in resource groups for easier administration.

- Leverage built-in tools like Cloud Shell and Azure Marketplace to accelerate work.
- Customize the experience to suit your workflow, team, or project needs.

In the next section, we will dive into deploying a virtual machine—a fundamental building block of cloud infrastructure—and explore hands-on experience with compute resources in Azure.

Deploying a Virtual Machine

Deploying a virtual machine (VM) is one of the most fundamental and versatile tasks in Microsoft Azure. Azure VMs allow users to run Windows or Linux operating systems in the cloud and provide scalable, on-demand compute power for development, testing, production, or training environments. Mastering VM deployment will give you critical insight into how Azure compute services operate, how resources are structured, and how infrastructure is managed at scale.

This section provides a comprehensive, hands-on walkthrough of deploying a virtual machine in Azure using the Portal, Azure CLI, and Resource Manager templates. We will also cover VM configuration, networking setup, storage options, cost control, monitoring, and cleanup practices.

Virtual Machine Overview

A virtual machine in Azure is a software emulation of a physical computer. You can install operating systems, run applications, and interact with it just like a local server. Azure supports a wide variety of VM sizes, operating systems, and configuration types.

Common Use Cases:

- Hosting websites and APIs
- Running enterprise applications
- Creating isolated development and test environments
- Learning Linux or Windows administration
- Running background jobs or services

Steps to Deploy a Virtual Machine via Azure Portal

1. Navigate to "Virtual Machines"

- Open the **Azure Portal** (https://portal.azure.com[7])
- Search for **Virtual Machines**
- Click **Create > Azure Virtual Machine**

2. Basics Configuration

- **Subscription**: Select your active subscription (e.g., Free Trial)
- **Resource group**: Create or select an existing resource group (e.g., vm-lab-rg)
- **Virtual machine name**: e.g., MyTestVM
- **Region**: Select a nearby region (e.g., UK South)
- **Availability options**: Use default (no redundancy) for trial

---

7. https://portal.azure.com/

- **Image**: Choose an OS (e.g., Windows Server 2019 or Ubuntu 20.04 LTS)
- **Size**: Click "See all sizes" and choose B1s (free tier eligible)
- **Username**: Create a local admin username
- **Authentication type**: Choose **password** or **SSH public key**
- **Inbound port rules**: Allow selected ports (e.g., RDP 3389 or SSH 22)

3. Disks Configuration

- **OS Disk Type**: Choose Standard SSD or Standard HDD to stay within free limits
- Leave default disk encryption enabled

4. Networking

- Virtual Network: Use existing or create new (e.g., vm-vnet)
- Subnet: Auto-generated or create custom (e.g., default)
- Public IP: Enable (dynamic or static)
- Network Security Group (NSG): Basic NSG with selected ports open

5. Management

- Enable **Boot diagnostics** (optional)
- Disable auto-shutdown (or configure to save credit)

- Enable **Azure Monitoring** if desired

6. Review + Create

- Review the summary
- Click **Create**

Azure will deploy the VM, allocate an IP address, configure storage and networking, and provision the OS.

Connect to the Virtual Machine

For Windows VMs (RDP):

- In the VM overview, click **Connect > RDP**
- Download the .rdp file and open it
- Log in with the credentials you created

For Linux VMs (SSH):

```
# If using SSH key:

ssh azureuser@<public-ip-address>
```

You now have console access to your cloud-hosted machine.

Deploying a Virtual Machine via Azure CLI

```
# Log in to Azure

az login

# Create a resource group
```

```
az group create—name vm-lab-rg—location uksouth

# Create a VM

az vm create \

—resource-group vm-lab-rg \

—name MyCLIVM \

—image UbuntuLTS \

—admin-username azureuser \

—generate-ssh-keys \

—size Standard_B1s
```

This command provisions a Linux VM using the Ubuntu LTS image, creates SSH keys, and assigns them to the VM.

Key VM Concepts and Components

Virtual Network (VNet)

- Required for network communication
- All VMs are connected to a subnet in a VNet

Network Security Group (NSG)

- Controls inbound/outbound traffic using firewall-like rules
- Rules are evaluated in priority order

OS Disk and Data Disks

- The OS disk holds the operating system
- You can add managed **data disks** for application data, logs, etc.

Public IP Address

- Optional; used for direct external access (e.g., RDP/SSH)

Managing the Virtual Machine

You can perform common VM management tasks directly from the Azure Portal or CLI:

Start/Stop VM:

az vm start—name MyCLIVM—resource-group vm-lab-rg

az vm deallocate—name MyCLIVM—resource-group vm-lab-rg

Resize the VM:

az vm resize \

—resource-group vm-lab-rg \

—name MyCLIVM \

—size Standard_B2s

Add a Data Disk:

az vm disk attach \

—vm-name MyCLIVM \

—resource-group vm-lab-rg \

—name MyDataDisk \

—new \

—size-gb 20

Monitor Usage:

- Go to VM → Monitoring → Metrics
- View CPU utilization, disk IOPS, and network throughput

Cost Management for VMs

Azure VMs are billed per second while running. Key ways to minimize costs:

1. **Deallocate VMs when not in use**
   - Only stopped (deallocated) VMs stop billing compute
2. **Use low-cost SKUs (e.g., B-series)**
3. **Enable auto-shutdown**
4. **Delete unused resources like disks and IPs**
5. **Use reserved instances for long-term workloads**

Auto-shutdown daily at 7 PM UTC

az vm auto-shutdown—resource-group vm-lab-rg—name MyCLIVM—time 1900

Clean Up Resources

After testing, delete all resources to avoid charges.

az group delete—name vm-lab-rg—yes—no-wait

This deletes the resource group and all associated resources (VM, network, disk, IP, etc.)

Summary

Deploying a virtual machine in Azure introduces key concepts in cloud compute, storage, and networking. It allows you to build real-world infrastructure quickly and test scenarios from development to enterprise workloads.

Key Takeaways:

- VMs can be deployed through the Portal, CLI, or templates.
- VM configurations include OS, size, authentication, networking, and disks.
- NSGs and VNets control traffic flow and access.
- Azure provides cost-saving options like shutdown scheduling and B-series SKUs.
- Always clean up resources after usage to avoid unexpected charges.

In the next section, we'll build on this foundation by creating a simple web app using Azure App Service—a powerful platform-as-a-service (PaaS) offering for developers.

Building a Simple Web App

One of the most powerful and accessible services in Azure is the **Azure App Service**, a Platform-as-a-Service (PaaS) offering that allows developers to quickly deploy and scale web applications without worrying about the underlying infrastructure. Azure App Service supports multiple programming languages and frameworks including .NET, Node.js, Python, Java, PHP, and more.

In this hands-on lab, you will learn how to create and deploy a simple web application using Azure App Service. You will also learn how to configure key settings such as scaling, authentication, deployment slots, monitoring, and cost management.

This exercise is essential preparation for real-world web application hosting and aligns directly with the AZ-900 exam objectives around core Azure services and application hosting platforms.

Introduction to Azure App Service

Azure App Service allows you to:

- Host web applications, RESTful APIs, and mobile backends.
- Use continuous integration/deployment from GitHub, Azure Repos, or other systems.
- Run applications on Windows or Linux using managed compute resources.
- Scale applications vertically or horizontally with minimal configuration.
- Add SSL certificates, custom domains, staging environments, and more.

Creating a Web App via Azure Portal

Step 1: Navigate to App Services

1. Go to the **Azure Portal**
2. Search for **App Services** in the global search bar
3. Click + **Create**

Step 2: Configure Basic Settings

- **Subscription**: Select your active subscription
- **Resource Group**: Create one or select an existing group (e.g., webapp-lab-rg)
- **Name**: Must be globally unique (e.g., myfirstazurewebapp123)
- **Publish**: Select **Code**
- **Runtime stack**: Choose a stack like .NET 6, Node.js, or Python 3.11
- **Operating System**: Choose **Windows** or **Linux**
- **Region**: Choose closest Azure region
- **App Service Plan**: Create a new one (e.g., webapp-plan)
    - Use F1 (Free Tier) for trial purposes

Click **Next** through the other configuration steps or leave defaults, then click **Review + Create** and then **Create**.

Deploying a Sample Application

After deployment, your web app is live at:

https://<app-name>.azurewebsites.net

You can deploy content using:

- **Azure Portal**
- **Azure CLI**
- **FTP**
- **Visual Studio / VS Code**
- **GitHub Actions**

Using Azure CLI to Deploy HTML Site

Create a simple index.html:

```
<!DOCTYPE html>
<html>
<head><title>Hello Azure</title></head>
<body><h1>My First Azure Web App</h1></body>
</html>
```

Then deploy it:

```
# Zip your content
zip site.zip index.html
# Upload to Azure
az webapp deployment source config-zip \
—resource-group webapp-lab-rg \
```

—name myfirstazurewebapp123 \

—src site.zip

Refresh your browser to view the site.

Managing the App Service

From the App Service blade, you can manage the following:

Configuration

- Set environment variables (Application settings)
- Customize the startup command (especially for Node.js or Python apps)

Scaling

- **Manual scale**: Change the number of instances
- **Autoscale**: Automatically increase/decrease based on CPU, memory, or request count

Scale to 2 instances

az appservice plan update \

—name webapp-plan \

—resource-group webapp-lab-rg \

—number-of-workers 2

Custom Domains and SSL

- Add a custom domain (e.g.,www.example.com[8])
- Upload or purchase an SSL certificate
- Configure HTTPS redirection

Deployment Slots

- Create a **staging slot** to test updates before pushing to production
- Swap slots with zero downtime deployment

Identity and Access

- Enable **Azure AD Authentication** for your app
- Protect routes or entire apps with enterprise identity

Monitoring and Diagnostics

Azure App Service provides built-in tools for logging and diagnostics:

- **Application Logging**: Save logs to file system or storage account
- **Web Server Logging**: Track request/response traffic
- **Detailed Error Messages**: Useful for debugging
- **Azure Monitor Integration**: Analyze performance and health
- **Application Insights**: Enable full observability with distributed tracing and telemetry

8. http://www.example.com/

```
# Enable logging
az webapp log config \
—name myfirstazurewebapp123 \
—resource-group webapp-lab-rg \
—application-logging filesystem \
—level information
```

Continuous Deployment from GitHub

Integrate GitHub for automated CI/CD:

1. In App Service, go to **Deployment Center**
2. Select **GitHub** > authorize Azure to access your GitHub account
3. Select repo and branch
4. Azure creates a GitHub Actions workflow for deployment

Azure rebuilds and deploys your app automatically when you push changes.

App Service Plan Considerations

Azure App Service runs your apps on **App Service Plans**, which define:

- Region
- Number of instances
- Tier (Free, Shared, Basic, Standard, Premium)
- Features like autoscale, staging, backups

Free (F1) Tier:

- 1 GB memory
- Shared compute
- Limited features (no custom domains, no scale out)

Upgrade to Standard or Premium for high availability, private networking, and autoscaling.

Clean-Up and Deletion

After completing this lab, delete unused resources to avoid charges.

az group delete—name webapp-lab-rg—yes—no-wait

This removes your web app, app service plan, storage, and other associated resources.

Summary

Azure App Service provides an easy, scalable, and cost-effective platform to host modern web applications with minimal management overhead. Whether you're deploying static sites or dynamic APIs, the platform supports multiple stacks, deployment methods, and enterprise-grade features.

Key Takeaways:

- Azure App Service simplifies web hosting using a fully managed platform.
- You can deploy code via CLI, portal, or CI/CD tools like GitHub Actions.

- App Services include diagnostics, autoscaling, custom domains, and secure identity.
- Free and shared tiers make it easy to experiment without costs.
- Proper use of deployment slots and scaling ensures zero-downtime and performance.

In the next section, we will use Azure Resource Manager to group and manage related resources more effectively and begin working with Infrastructure-as-Code principles to streamline future deployments.

Practicing with Azure Resource Groups

Azure Resource Groups are fundamental building blocks for managing resources in Microsoft Azure. A resource group acts as a logical container that holds related Azure resources such as virtual machines, web apps, databases, storage accounts, and networking interfaces. Organizing your resources within groups improves manageability, enhances governance, and provides control over costs, access, and lifecycle.

In this hands-on section, you will practice using Azure Resource Groups through the Azure Portal and Azure CLI. You will learn to create, organize, tag, monitor, and clean up resources efficiently. By mastering this foundational skill, you'll be better equipped to structure your Azure environment and prepare for both the AZ-900 certification and real-world cloud administration.

What is a Resource Group?

A **Resource Group** is a container for resources deployed on Azure. All resources must reside in a resource group, and each resource group exists within a subscription.

Key Properties:

- Can contain resources from multiple regions.
- Resources in a group can be managed collectively.
- Supports RBAC (Role-Based Access Control) at the group level.
- Acts as a boundary for applying policies and tagging strategies.

Best Practice: Group resources that share the same lifecycle. For example, all resources supporting a single application or workload.

Creating a Resource Group via the Azure Portal

1. **Log in to the Azure Portal**:https://portal.azure.com[9]
2. In the left-hand menu, select **Resource Groups**
3. Click + **Create**
4. **Basics**:
    - **Subscription**: Choose your active subscription
    - **Resource Group Name**: Example: dev-lab-rg
    - **Region**: Choose the region closest to your users or project

---

9. https://portal.azure.com/

5. Click **Review + Create** and then **Create**

Once created, you'll be directed to the overview screen, where you can begin adding resources to the group.

Creating a Resource Group via Azure CLI

Create a new resource group in West Europe

az group create \

—name dev-lab-rg \

—location westeurope

You can verify creation with:

az group show—name dev-lab-rg

To list all resource groups:

az group list—output table

Deploying Resources into a Resource Group

All Azure resources must be created within a resource group. Here are examples of how to deploy resources into your group:

Create a Storage Account:

az storage account create \

—name mystorageaccdemo \

—resource-group dev-lab-rg \

—location westeurope \

—sku Standard_LRS

Create an App Service Plan:

az appservice plan create \

—name demoAppPlan \

—resource-group dev-lab-rg \

—sku F1 \

—is-linux

Create a Web App:

az webapp create \

—name demowebapp12345 \

—resource-group dev-lab-rg \

—plan demoAppPlan \

—runtime "NODE|18-lts"

All these resources will now appear within your resource group in the Azure Portal.

Managing Resource Groups

Tagging Resources

Tags allow you to categorize and track resources based on attributes like cost center, environment, or owner.

Add tags to a resource group

az group update \

—name dev-lab-rg \

—tags Environment=Development Owner=jane.doe@domain.com

Use the Azure Portal to view and edit tags by navigating to the "Tags" section of the resource group.

Moving Resources

You can move resources between groups or subscriptions:

- In the Portal: Go to the resource → "Move" → "Move to another resource group"
- CLI:

az resource move \

—destination-group new-rg-name \

—ids /subscriptions/<id>/resourceGroups/dev-lab-rg/providers/Microsoft.Web/sites/demowebapp12345

Note: Some resources have limitations or dependencies that may prevent moving.

Access Control with RBAC

You can assign user roles at the resource group level to control access:

In the Portal:

1. Navigate to the resource group
2. Click **Access control (IAM)**
3. Click + **Add** > **Add role assignment**
4. Select a role (e.g., Contributor), user, and assign

CLI:

az role assignment create \

—assignee user@domain.com \

—role Contributor \

—resource-group dev-lab-rg

This allows for scoped access, avoiding over-provisioning users at the subscription level.

Monitoring and Usage

The Azure Portal provides rich monitoring tools under the "Activity log" and "Metrics" sections of a resource group.

• **Activity log** shows administrative operations such as creation, deletion, and access.

• **Metrics** allow you to visualize aggregated data for all resources in the group.

This helps in understanding usage patterns, troubleshooting, and validating automation.

Automating Resource Group Deployments

You can define infrastructure using ARM templates or Bicep files and deploy them to a resource group:

ARM Template Deployment:

```
az deployment group create \

—resource-group dev-lab-rg \

—template-file azuredeploy.json \

—parameters azuredeploy.parameters.json
```

Bicep Example:

```
resource storage 'Microsoft.Storage/storageAccounts@2022-09-01' = {

name: 'demostorageacc123'

location: resourceGroup().location

sku: {

name: 'Standard_LRS'

}

kind: 'StorageV2'

}
```

Bicep allows concise, modular, and repeatable deployments ideal for enterprise-scale infrastructure.

Deleting Resource Groups

When you're finished with a lab or environment, you can delete the entire resource group:

az group delete—name dev-lab-rg—yes—no-wait

This will recursively delete all resources contained within it. Use this to ensure no orphaned or chargeable resources remain active.

Best Practices for Resource Group Management

1. **Group by lifecycle**: Place resources with shared lifecycles in the same group.
2. **Apply tags consistently**: Use automation to enforce tagging.
3. **Scope policies and roles**: Use groups as boundaries for access control and governance.
4. **Use naming conventions**: Ensure clarity across teams with structured naming (e.g., <env>-<service>-<region>).
5. **Monitor activity**: Enable diagnostic logs and track administrative actions.
6. **Automate**: Leverage templates and deployment scripts for consistency.

Summary

Azure Resource Groups provide structure, visibility, and control over your cloud environment. By practicing their creation and management, you lay a strong foundation for working effectively in Azure, whether deploying manually or using automation.

Key Takeaways:

- Resource groups logically organize related resources.
- They serve as boundaries for access, billing, and lifecycle management.
- Tags, RBAC, and policies are scoped at the resource group level.
- Resources can be moved, grouped, and deleted with ease.
- Using automation (ARM, Bicep, Terraform) ensures repeatability and governance.

With resource group management skills in place, you're now equipped to work efficiently across a variety of Azure services. In the next chapter, we'll shift focus toward AZ-900 exam readiness strategies and test-taking tips to solidify your knowledge and prepare for certification success.

Chapter 7: Exam Readiness and Test-Taking Tips

Reviewing the AZ-900 Skills Measured

The AZ-900: Microsoft Azure Fundamentals certification exam is designed for individuals beginning their journey into cloud computing. The exam assesses foundational-level knowledge of cloud services and how those services are provided with Microsoft Azure. To successfully pass the AZ-900, it is critical to have a structured understanding of the key skill areas measured in the exam, how they are weighted, and the types of topics each domain encompasses.

This section provides a deep dive into the official skills measured, breaks them down into categories, aligns them with chapters covered earlier in this book, and offers study tips and review strategies to maximize exam readiness.

Microsoft's Official Exam Outline

As of the latest Microsoft Learn documentation, the AZ-900 exam focuses on the following domains:

Skill Area	Exam Weight
Describe cloud concepts	25–30%
Describe core Azure services	15–20%
Describe core solutions and management tools on Azure	10–15%
Describe general security and network security features	10–15%
Describe identity, governance, privacy, and compliance	20–25%
Describe Azure cost management and Service Level Agreements (SLAs)	10–15%

These domains form the backbone of your study strategy and map directly to the structure of this book.

Mapping Chapters to Exam Objectives

Use the following table to correlate book chapters to official exam sections for efficient review:

Exam Objective	Relevant Book Chapter(s)
Describe cloud concepts	Chapter 2
Describe core Azure services	Chapter 3
Describe core solutions and management tools on Azure	Chapter 3, Chapter 6
Describe general security and network security features	Chapter 4
Describe identity, governance, privacy, and compliance	Chapter 4
Describe Azure cost management and SLAs	Chapter 5

Aligning your review to this structure ensures a thorough and targeted study process.

Domain 1: Describe Cloud Concepts (25–30%)

This domain emphasizes foundational knowledge:

- Benefits of cloud computing (cost, agility, scalability)
- Cloud models: public, private, hybrid
- Cloud service types: IaaS, PaaS, SaaS
- Shared responsibility model

Focus Areas:

- Understand real-world cloud adoption drivers
- Distinguish service models by use cases
- Use analogies (e.g., renting a car vs. owning) to reinforce understanding

Tip: Expect scenario-based questions that require identifying the best cloud model or service type.

Domain 2: Describe Core Azure Services (15–20%)

Key concepts include:

- Core Azure architectural components (regions, availability zones, resource groups)
- Compute services (VMs, App Services, AKS, Functions)
- Networking (VNets, Load Balancer, Application Gateway)
- Storage (Blob, File, Disk, Tables)

Tip: Be familiar with icons and service purposes. For instance, know that Azure Functions support serverless compute, while Azure Virtual Machines offer IaaS.

Practice: Use the Azure Portal or CLI to deploy basic services like VMs and storage accounts.

Domain 3: Describe Core Solutions and Management Tools on Azure (10–15%)

Topics include:

- IoT, Machine Learning, AI, DevOps (Azure DevOps, GitHub Actions)

- Management tools (Azure Portal, CLI, PowerShell, ARM templates, Cloud Shell)

- Monitoring solutions (Azure Monitor, Application Insights)

Strategy:

- Don't focus deeply on implementation. Understand **when** and **why** you'd use each tool or solution.

- Know that ARM templates provide infrastructure as code, and Cloud Shell enables quick CLI access.

Domain 4: Describe General Security and Network Security Features (10–15%)

This domain addresses Azure security offerings:

- Security tools (Microsoft Defender for Cloud, Sentinel)

- Network security (NSGs, firewalls, DDoS protection)

- Identity protection (MFA, Conditional Access)

Review Focus:

- Know the **purpose** of each tool rather than implementation details.

- Understand how services like Azure Firewall differ from NSGs.

Memory Aid: NSGs control traffic at the network interface/subnet level; Azure Firewall is a centralized, stateful firewall for broader scenarios.

Domain 5: Describe Identity, Governance, Privacy, and Compliance (20–25%)

Key concepts:

- Azure Active Directory

- Role-Based Access Control (RBAC)

- Azure Policy, Blueprints

- Compliance tools (Compliance Manager, Trust Center)

- Data protection principles (encryption, data residency, GDPR)

Tips:

- Review real-life identity scenarios: assigning roles, enforcing MFA, using managed identities.

- Know the purpose of governance tools and where to apply them.

Practice: Assign a reader role to a user via the Azure Portal or CLI.

Domain 6: Describe Azure Cost Management and

SLAs (10–15%)

Important areas:

- Azure Pricing Calculator
- TCO Calculator
- Cost Management and Billing
- Budgets, alerts, and tagging
- Service Level Agreements (SLAs) and composite SLA calculation

Must Know:

- Cost control mechanisms: budgets, alerts, reservations
- How SLAs are calculated and the difference between individual and composite SLAs

Formula:

Composite SLA = SLA1 x SLA2 x SLA3

Using Microsoft Learn and Practice Resources

Microsoft Learn provides free, interactive modules directly aligned with AZ-900:

- https://learn.microsoft.com/en-us/training/paths/azure-fundamentals/

Use sandbox environments to complete labs without consuming your own subscription.

Practice Tests:

- Microsoft Official Practice Tests
- MeasureUp (endorsed by Microsoft)
- Whizlabs, ExamTopics (community-based)

Tip: Take multiple practice tests to expose gaps and reinforce recall under time pressure.

Time Management and Review Techniques

1. **Skim-reinforce-deep dive method**:
   - Skim each domain's key terms
   - Reinforce with portal exploration
   - Deep dive into unfamiliar or unclear topics
2. **Flashcards** for services and abbreviations (e.g., RBAC, NSG, SLA)
3. **Daily review habit**:
   - 30 minutes: one domain
   - 10 minutes: past domain recap
   - 5 minutes: quick quiz or self-test

Summary

The AZ-900 exam requires a broad yet shallow understanding of Azure's core services, pricing, security, and cloud principles. By reviewing the measured skills in a structured and consistent way, you'll improve your retention, build confidence, and increase your likelihood of success.

Key Takeaways:

- Focus on why services exist and when to use them, not how to configure them.
- Use Microsoft Learn for hands-on practice with zero cost.
- Understand service categories, identity roles, cost tools, and governance models.
- Reinforce concepts using CLI/Portal exercises covered in earlier chapters.
- Use practice exams to simulate real test conditions and reduce anxiety.

The next section will guide you through a full practice test walkthrough, helping you apply this knowledge in an exam-style format and identify final areas to review.

Practice Test Walkthrough

One of the most effective methods to reinforce knowledge and prepare for the AZ-900 exam is to complete structured practice tests that simulate the real exam environment. A comprehensive walkthrough of sample questions helps you understand the question styles, apply concepts from multiple domains in context, and develop strategic approaches for answering scenario-based and multi-select items. This section provides a complete, guided practice test walkthrough with detailed explanations for each question and option, highlighting test-taking strategies that maximize success.

The practice questions presented here are not replicas of the actual AZ-900 exam but are aligned with the official exam objectives and designed to mirror its format, coverage, and difficulty level.

Question 1: Cloud Benefits

Which of the following is a benefit of cloud computing?

A. Increased capital expenditure

B. Inconsistent performance across tenants

C. High availability

D. Manual scaling of infrastructure

Correct Answer: C. High availability

Explanation:

High availability ensures that cloud services remain operational with minimal downtime, a core benefit of cloud platforms like Azure. The cloud enables redundancy across regions, availability zones, and services. Option A is incorrect because cloud computing reduces capital expenditure in favor of operational expenditure. Option B is false as Azure aims for consistency. Option D is incorrect because scaling is typically automatic.

Question 2: Azure Service Types

Which Azure service type allows you to manage VMs without worrying about the underlying infrastructure?

A. IaaS

B. SaaS

C. PaaS

D. Virtual Network

Correct Answer: C. PaaS

Explanation:

Platform-as-a-Service (PaaS) abstracts away the infrastructure layer, allowing developers to focus on building apps. IaaS still requires managing VMs and networking. SaaS delivers fully functional applications. Virtual Network is a resource, not a service model.

Question 3: Azure Regions and Availability

What is the purpose of Azure Availability Zones?

A. Provide multi-tenancy for VMs

B. Isolate workloads for compliance purposes

C. Ensure high availability by distributing workloads across physically separate data centers

D. Reduce the cost of virtual machine deployment

Correct Answer: C. Ensure high availability by distributing workloads across physically separate data centers

Explanation:

Availability Zones are distinct physical locations within an Azure region, each with independent power, cooling, and networking. They're used to improve fault tolerance and resilience.

Question 4: Azure Identity Management

Which feature allows a service like a VM to securely access other Azure resources without storing credentials?

A. Azure Active Directory B2C

B. Service Principal

C. Managed Identity

D. Azure Policy

Correct Answer: C. Managed Identity

Explanation:

Managed Identities provide Azure resources with an automatically managed identity in Azure AD. This enables authentication without secrets. Service principals require manual credential handling. B2C is for customer identity management. Azure Policy enforces compliance.

Question 5: Cost Optimization

Which tool helps you forecast Azure spending and set spending limits?

A. Azure DevTest Labs

B. Azure TCO Calculator

C. Azure Cost Management + Billing

D. Azure Advisor only

Correct Answer: C. Azure Cost Management + Billing

Explanation:

Azure Cost Management enables you to track resource usage, forecast spending, and define budgets and alerts. The TCO calculator compares on-prem and cloud costs but doesn't track live usage. Advisor offers cost recommendations but lacks budgeting features.

Question 6: Shared Responsibility

In the shared responsibility model, what is the customer responsible for when using Azure PaaS?

A. Physical datacenter security

B. Network cabling and hardware

C. Application data and access

D. Hypervisor patching

Correct Answer: C. Application data and access

Explanation:

In PaaS, Microsoft manages infrastructure, OS, and platform services, while the customer manages app logic, access controls, and data integrity.

Question 7: Azure Compliance

Which of the following provides a detailed view of Microsoft compliance offerings, audits, and certifications?

A. Azure Portal

B. Microsoft Trust Center

C. Azure Advisor

D. Azure Blueprints

Correct Answer: B. Microsoft Trust Center

Explanation:

The Microsoft Trust Center provides transparency on Azure's compliance status with global standards and certifications. Azure Advisor and Blueprints are for recommendations and deployment governance.

Question 8: SLA Calculation

You build a solution using three services with individual SLAs of 99.9%, 99.95%, and 99.99%. What is the composite SLA?

A. 99.9%

B. 99.999%

C. 99.84%

D. 99.7%

Correct Answer: C. 99.84%

Explanation:

Composite SLA is calculated by multiplying the individual availability rates:

$0.999 \times 0.9995 \times 0.9999 \approx 0.9984 \rightarrow 99.84\%$

Question 9: Networking Security

What does a Network Security Group (NSG) do?

A. Encrypts outbound traffic

B. Monitors user behavior

C. Defines traffic rules to allow or deny traffic to resources

D. Routes traffic to express route circuits

Correct Answer: C. Defines traffic rules to allow or deny traffic to resources

Explanation:

NSGs act as firewall rules for Azure resources. They don't perform monitoring (that's Azure Monitor) or encryption.

Question 10: Application Hosting

Which Azure service is best suited for hosting a web application without managing infrastructure?

A. Azure Virtual Machine

B. Azure Kubernetes Service

C. Azure App Service

D. Azure Functions

Correct Answer: C. Azure App Service

Explanation:

App Service is designed to host web apps with minimal overhead. Azure Functions is more suited for event-driven tasks. AKS and VMs require infrastructure management.

Scoring and Evaluation

To assess your performance:

- 8–10 correct: Ready for the exam
- 6–7 correct: Review weak areas and retry practice tests
- Below 6: Revisit relevant chapters and redo hands-on labs

Use incorrect answers as learning opportunities. Document the reasoning behind your mistakes and reinforce those concepts through labs or Microsoft Learn modules.

Common Question Types in the Exam

1. **Single correct choice**
2. **Multiple correct choices**
3. **Yes/No scenario**
4. **Drag and drop**
5. **Case studies**

Tip: Read each question carefully. Look for absolutes like "always," "never," or "only," which often indicate incorrect choices.

Final Review Strategy

- Complete multiple practice tests from varied sources
- Review explanations, not just answers
- Focus on weak areas (e.g., SLAs, service models, identity)
- Practice using Azure Portal and CLI for real-world alignment

Example practice CLI usage:

az group create—name myReviewGroup—location uksouth

az webapp list—query "[].{name:name, state:state}"—output table

Summary

A structured practice test experience is critical for identifying knowledge gaps and solidifying your understanding of core Azure concepts. Practice tests mimic the real exam environment and promote retention by encouraging active recall.

Key Takeaways:

- Practice exams reinforce learning and reduce test anxiety.
- Focus on the reasoning behind correct and incorrect answers.
- Identify weak domains and revisit them with hands-on labs or Microsoft Learn modules.
- Understand key calculation methods (e.g., composite SLA).
- Simulate exam conditions for timing and pacing awareness.

The next section will provide advanced strategies for managing your time during the exam and how to approach each question type efficiently to maximize your score under real test conditions.

Time Management During the Exam

Time management is one of the most overlooked yet critical aspects of passing the AZ-900: Microsoft Azure Fundamentals certification exam. While the exam covers introductory-level knowledge, its success requires more than just technical familiarity—it also demands strategic allocation of time across questions, managing stress, pacing correctly, and making smart decisions about question navigation.

This section covers techniques and frameworks for managing time efficiently during the AZ-900 exam. It includes practical examples, question-type strategies, pacing plans, and cognitive techniques to reduce errors and maximize your score within the allotted time.

AZ-900 Exam Format and Timing

Official Exam Overview:

- **Duration:** 60 minutes (exam timer)
- **Total Allotted Time:** 85 minutes (includes setup and survey)
- **Number of Questions:** 40–60 (varies per candidate)
- **Question Types:** Multiple-choice, drag-and-drop, hot area, case studies, true/false
- **Passing Score:** 700 out of 1000
- **Scoring System:** No penalty for incorrect answers; only correct answers contribute to the score

---

Optimal Time Allocation Strategy

Assuming a typical exam length of 50 questions, you have roughly:

- **1.2 minutes per question** (72 seconds)
- **10 minutes buffer** for reviewing marked questions
- **5 minutes for survey/instructions**

Pacing Benchmarks:

Exam Progress	Time Elapsed	Questions Completed
After 10 minutes	8–10	Keep pace early
After 30 minutes	25–30	Midpoint check
After 50 minutes	45–50	Final few

Staying within these checkpoints helps prevent time bottlenecks at the end, which often leads to rushed guesses and preventable mistakes.

The Three-Pass Technique

One of the most effective ways to handle questions is the **Three-Pass Technique**:

Pass 1: Fast Filter (0.5–1 min per question)

- Answer the easy and familiar questions first.
- Mark difficult or long questions for later.
- Don't overthink—go with your first confident answer.

Pass 2: Moderate Review (1–1.5 min per marked question)

- Revisit marked questions with remaining time.
- Re-read the question and eliminate wrong options.
- Apply logic and exam objectives knowledge.

Pass 3: Final Audit (Remaining time)

- Rapidly review answers to questions you're still unsure of.
- Avoid changing correct answers unless you're sure.
- Ensure no questions are left blank.

Reading the Question Strategically

Efficient time management begins with **strategic reading**:

- **Read the last sentence first.** It often reveals the exact question.
- **Scan for keywords:** "best", "most cost-effective", "secure", "true/false"
- **Eliminate extremes:** Choices with words like "always", "only", "never" are often incorrect.
- **Beware of distractors:** Azure exams frequently include tempting answers that are partially correct.

Example Tip:

"Which Azure service should you use to host a scalable web application with minimal infrastructure management?"

- Eliminate VMs (requires infra mgmt)
- Consider App Service (PaaS)—likely correct

This saves valuable seconds otherwise spent second-guessing.

Question Types and Time Tactics

Single-Select Multiple Choice:

- Most common
- Use elimination quickly
- Spend no more than 45–60 seconds

Multi-Select (Choose all that apply):

- Read if it says "Select two" or "Select all that apply"
- Use logic to narrow down
- Aim for <90 seconds

Drag-and-Drop / Hot Area:

- Visual questions
- Match concepts or steps in the correct order
- Watch out for trick options or duplicates
- Aim for <1.5 minutes

Case Studies:

- Longer questions with several sub-questions
- You'll have a reference tab with the case scenario
- Allocate 5–8 minutes for an entire case

- Don't reread the case for every sub-question—take notes or use the scratchpad

Yes/No Questions:

- Common in Microsoft exams
- Usually test your ability to validate a statement against Azure features
- Use decision trees or short definitions in your mind
- Take <30 seconds

Managing Stress and Cognitive Load

Efficient time management is as much about **mental control** as it is about pacing:

- **Skip the first difficult question**: Don't let early blockers ruin your confidence
- **Use the on-screen scratchpad** (or paper, if testing center): Write down confusing terms, services, or calculations
- **Don't panic at the clock**: Trust your pace and pass method
- **Reframe nerves as focus**: Moderate stress increases alertness

Use calming breathing patterns: Inhale 4 seconds, hold 4, exhale 4—especially helpful when moving into a case study or after a tough question.

Common Time Traps to Avoid

- **Over-reading**: Don't read the scenario more than twice unless essential.

- **Second-guessing everything**: Stick with your first choice unless evidence tells you otherwise.

- **Fixation on one question**: If you spend >2 minutes, flag and move on.

- **Changing too many answers at the end**: Often leads to lower accuracy.

Tools You Can Use During the Exam

- **Flag/Mark for Review**: Click the flag icon to return later

- **Back/Next Navigation**: You can usually go back unless it's a locked case

- **Highlight Feature**: Use to isolate keywords in complex questions

- **On-screen Calculator**: Available for basic math and conversions (e.g., uptime calculations)

- **Scratchpad**: Digital or paper notes (depending on test format)

Practice with a Timer

Use a countdown timer app or exam simulator set to 60 minutes with 50 questions. This helps develop muscle memory for timing, increases confidence, and familiarizes you with pressure pacing.

Sample Timing Practice Schedule:

Task	Duration
First 25 questions	25 mins
Remaining 25	25 mins
Final review	10 mins

Simulate the environment: silence, no distractions, no breaks.

Summary

Time management during the AZ-900 exam is essential for maximizing performance, minimizing errors, and navigating confidently through all question types. By applying a structured pacing strategy, recognizing traps, and remaining calm under pressure, you can efficiently allocate time to every question and improve your chances of passing on your first attempt.

Key Takeaways:

- Allocate an average of 1.2 minutes per question.
- Use the Three-Pass Technique: fast pass, moderate review, final audit.
- Read strategically, eliminate wrong answers fast, and move forward.
- Practice under timed conditions before the exam.
- Don't dwell on hard questions early—mark and return.
- Use built-in tools like the flag option, calculator, and scratchpad.
- Maintain composure and focus with breath control and pacing benchmarks.

The final section of this chapter will help you handle trick questions, word traps, and advanced exam scenarios where phrasing, nuance, and contextual clues play a decisive role in selecting the correct answer.

Handling Trick Questions and Scenarios

The AZ-900: Microsoft Azure Fundamentals certification exam, although foundational in nature, is strategically designed to test your conceptual clarity, situational awareness, and decision-making skills. Many candidates lose critical points not due to a lack of knowledge, but because of **misreading**, **falling for traps**, or **overlooking key nuances** in questions. This section focuses on **how to handle trick questions**, recognize **red flags**, and develop the cognitive precision required to choose the right answer under time pressure.

We will dissect various types of "trick" questions commonly found on the exam, provide real-world examples, offer strategies for navigating nuanced wording, and help you build confidence in choosing between closely related answer choices.

Understanding the Purpose of Trick Questions

Trick questions are not designed to trick you maliciously—they are designed to test:

- Your **attention to detail**
- Your understanding of **Azure terminology**
- Your ability to **distinguish between similar services**
- Your grasp of **Microsoft's best practices**

- Your skill in interpreting **key adjectives like "best," "most cost-effective," "automated," "secure," etc.**

To overcome these, you need more than rote memorization. You need applied, practical understanding and language-awareness.

Common Traps and How to Handle Them

1. The "Too Many Correct Answers" Trap

Question:

"Which Azure services support automated scaling?"

Options:

- A. Azure Virtual Machines
- B. Azure App Service
- C. Azure Kubernetes Service
- D. Azure Blob Storage

All seem plausible, but only some implement **native autoscale** functionality.

Correct Answers: B and C

- App Service: Native PaaS autoscaling
- AKS: Autoscaling via Kubernetes controllers
- Virtual Machines: Require manual scaling unless configured via VMSS

- Blob Storage: Doesn't involve "scaling compute," only storage capacity

Strategy:

- Identify which answers satisfy **all keywords** in the question.
- Eliminate answers that require additional configuration not mentioned.

---

2. The "Best" or "Most Appropriate" Wording Trap

Question:

"What is the most cost-effective solution for hosting a low-traffic static website?"

Options:

- A. Azure Kubernetes Service
- B. Azure Static Web Apps
- C. Azure App Service (Standard Plan)
- D. Azure Virtual Machines

Correct Answer: B

Explanation:

- The keyword is "**cost-effective**" and "**static website.**"
- AKS and VMs are excessive and expensive.
- App Service (Standard) adds cost and dynamic capability you don't need.

Strategy:

- Always align your selection with keywords like **cost-effective**, **simple**, or **scalable**.
- Avoid over-engineering.

---

3. Reverse Logic / Double Negatives

Question:

"Which of the following does **not** provide platform-level managed scaling?"

Options:

- A. Azure App Service
- B. Azure Functions
- C. Azure Virtual Machine Scale Sets
- D. Azure Virtual Machines

Correct Answer: D

Explanation:

- Virtual Machines are user-managed and require manual scaling unless integrated into VMSS.
- All others are PaaS/serverless and support managed scaling.

Strategy:

- **Circle or highlight** words like "not", "except", or "only".
- Rephrase the question in your own words if necessary.

---

4. Service Confusion Trap

Many services sound alike but serve different purposes.

Example: Azure Monitor vs. Azure Advisor

Question:

"Which service provides recommendations to reduce Azure costs and improve reliability?"

Correct Answer: Azure Advisor

- Azure Monitor provides logs, metrics, and alerting—not cost recommendations.

Comparison Strategy Table:

Feature	Azure Advisor	Azure Monitor
Cost Recommendations	◈	◈
Performance Suggestions	◈	◈
Metrics & Logs	◈	◈
Integration with Alerts	◈	◈

Tip: Build visual mnemonics or comparison tables in your notebook.

Microsoft-Specific Language Cues

Microsoft often embeds its own terminology in a way that defines the correct answer.

Common Keywords and What They Imply:

Keyword	Implication
"Cost-effective"	Use free/shared tiers or minimal overhead solutions
"Secure by default"	Services like Azure Key Vault, Defender for Cloud
"Scalable"	Look for PaaS or serverless options
"Platform-managed"	Exclude IaaS solutions
"Integrated with Azure AD"	Usually rules out older or less secure services
"Low maintenance"	Points toward PaaS/SaaS rather than VMs

Strategy: Reframe the question:

"If I had to explain this in plain English, what's being asked?"

Then revisit the options with fresh clarity.

Tactics for Complex or Case-Based Questions

1. Summarize Long Scenarios

- Don't get overwhelmed. Skim the case.
- Find the actual question prompt first.
- Highlight key details like: number of users, cost constraints, compliance needs.

2. Prioritize Constraints

If a question includes multiple constraints:

"Secure, scalable, and integrates with Azure AD..."

Eliminate answers that fail even **one** of the constraints.

3. Use Elimination with Confidence

Even if you don't know the answer immediately:

- Rule out obviously wrong options
- Choose the best remaining option—not the perfect one

Practicing for Trick Scenarios

Build muscle memory for these traps by:

- Doing timed practice exams with explanations
- Using Microsoft Learn and sandbox environments to test ideas
- Writing your own questions and having others answer them

Example Practice Question:

"You need to analyze login trends and detect anomalies in sign-in attempts across Azure AD. What should you use?"

- A. Azure Security Center
- B. Azure Monitor
- C. Azure Active Directory Sign-in Logs
- D. Microsoft Defender for Endpoint

Correct Answer: C

Only Azure AD sign-in logs provide authentication activity at that granularity.

Final Checkpoints During Exam

Before submitting, ask yourself:

1. Did I **answer all questions**? No blanks.
2. Did I **revisit flagged items** with fresh logic?
3. Did I avoid unnecessary changes to answers I was confident about?
4. Did I read "**not**," "**only**," and qualifiers carefully?
5. Do I feel confident about at least 70% of the answers?

If you've done all the above—trust yourself and submit.

Summary

Handling trick questions in the AZ-900 exam is about developing reading precision, avoiding cognitive traps, and applying your conceptual knowledge critically. By practicing under realistic conditions, staying aware of Microsoft's exam design language, and focusing on question intent rather than surface familiarity, you'll build the skillset to confidently navigate even the most nuanced scenarios.

Key Takeaways:

- Always identify and underline exam keywords like "not," "most appropriate," or "cost-effective."

- Break down complex or multi-choice questions by eliminating incorrect options.

- Use real-world logic aligned with Microsoft's cloud philosophy.

- Understand how services compare—use flashcards or tables to reinforce.

- Don't second-guess correct answers unless you find new, compelling evidence.

- The correct answer is not always the most powerful or feature-rich—it's the best **fit** for the specific scenario.

With strategic awareness and deliberate practice, even the trickiest AZ-900 questions become navigable. You're now fully prepared to walk into the exam center—or launch your online exam—with confidence and clarity.

Chapter 8: Appendices

Glossary of Terms

This glossary compiles and defines essential terms used throughout your preparation for the AZ-900: Microsoft Azure Fundamentals certification exam. It serves as a quick reference guide to clarify concepts, technologies, acronyms, and services that you've encountered in prior chapters. A firm grasp of this terminology is crucial not only for passing the exam but also for laying a strong foundation in cloud computing with Azure.

A

Active Directory (AD):

Microsoft's directory service for identity management. In Azure, Azure Active Directory (Azure AD) is used for authentication and access control in cloud environments.

ARM (Azure Resource Manager):

Azure's deployment and management service that provides a consistent management layer for resource provisioning through templates, CLI, SDKs, or the portal.

Availability Set:

A configuration that ensures high availability by distributing virtual machines across multiple physical servers, compute racks, and storage units within a datacenter.

Availability Zone:

Physically separate datacenters within an Azure region that offer redundancy and fault tolerance.

B

BLOB Storage (Binary Large Object):

Object storage solution in Azure for storing massive amounts of unstructured data like images, videos, backups, and logs.

Blueprints (Azure Blueprints):

A governance tool that helps deploy and maintain compliant environments by packaging policies, role assignments, resource groups, and templates.

C

Cloud Computing:

The delivery of computing services over the internet, including servers, storage, databases, networking, software, and analytics.

Cloud Shell:

A browser-accessible shell for managing Azure resources using CLI or PowerShell, with built-in tools and persistent storage.

Compliance Manager:

A Microsoft 365 tool that helps track compliance against regulatory standards using prebuilt assessment templates.

Content Delivery Network (CDN):

A distributed network of servers that delivers content such as webpages, videos, and scripts to users based on geographic proximity.

Cost Management + Billing:

A set of tools in Azure to track, analyze, and manage cloud spending through budgets, cost analysis, and recommendations.

D

Data Lake:

A scalable repository that stores raw, structured, and unstructured data for analytics and big data workloads.

DevOps:

A set of practices that combines software development (Dev) and IT operations (Ops) to shorten the system development lifecycle.

Disaster Recovery:

A strategy and process to recover applications and data after a catastrophic failure. Azure offers tools like Site Recovery for this purpose.

E

Elasticity:

The ability of cloud services to automatically scale up or down to accommodate workload demands.

Encryption at Rest / In Transit:

Techniques to secure data when stored (at rest) or transmitted (in transit) across a network using cryptographic methods.

F

Failover:

The process of automatically switching to a redundant or standby system in the event of a system failure.

Firewall (Azure Firewall):

A managed, cloud-based network security service that protects Azure Virtual Network resources.

G

Geography:

A geopolitical boundary used by Microsoft to determine data residency and compliance, containing multiple regions.

Governance:

A collection of mechanisms including policies, role assignments, and blueprints that help manage and control Azure resources effectively.

H

High Availability (HA):

Designing systems to ensure minimal downtime and maximum operational uptime through redundancy and failover mechanisms.

Hybrid Cloud:

A computing environment that combines public cloud and on-premises infrastructures, enabling data and application portability.

I

IaaS (Infrastructure as a Service):

A cloud computing model where virtualized computing resources are provided over the internet, including VMs, networking, and storage.

Identity and Access Management (IAM):

The practice of assigning and controlling user access and privileges to cloud resources through systems like Azure AD.

K

Key Vault:

An Azure service used to securely store and manage secrets, keys, and certificates.

L

Load Balancer:

A networking solution that distributes incoming traffic among healthy instances of an application or service to ensure high availability and scalability.

Lifecycle:

Refers to the stages of an Azure service or resource—from preview to general availability, updates, deprecation, and retirement.

M

Managed Identity:

An identity created and managed by Azure that allows services to authenticate to other Azure services without storing credentials.

Marketplace (Azure Marketplace):

An online store for preconfigured applications and services that can be deployed to Azure.

Monitoring (Azure Monitor):

A comprehensive solution for collecting, analyzing, and acting on telemetry from your cloud and on-premises environments.

N

NSG (Network Security Group):

A set of security rules that control inbound and outbound traffic to Azure resources within a virtual network.

NoSQL:

A type of non-relational database optimized for scalable and distributed data storage, often used with services like Cosmos DB.

O

Operational Expenditure (OpEx):

Ongoing cost for running cloud services. Unlike CapEx, it doesn't require heavy upfront investments.

P

PaaS (Platform as a Service):

A cloud model that delivers development and deployment tools on top of cloud infrastructure, relieving developers of infrastructure management.

Pricing Calculator:

An online tool provided by Azure to estimate costs based on selected services, configurations, and usage patterns.

Private Endpoint:

A network interface that connects you privately and securely to Azure services over the Azure backbone network.

R

RBAC (Role-Based Access Control):

A system for assigning permissions to users based on their roles to control access to Azure resources.

Region:

A set of data centers deployed within a specific geographic area that provides redundancy and latency benefits.

Resource Group:

A container for managing and organizing related Azure resources that share a common lifecycle.

S

SaaS (Software as a Service):

A cloud model where software is hosted and maintained by a provider, with access offered over the internet (e.g., Microsoft 365).

Service Level Agreement (SLA):

A formal contract that defines the guaranteed availability and performance standards of an Azure service.

Security Center (Microsoft Defender for Cloud):

A unified infrastructure security management system that strengthens security posture and protects against threats.

T

Tagging:

Attaching metadata to Azure resources for classification, organization, and cost management.

Total Cost of Ownership (TCO) Calculator:

A tool to estimate the cost savings of moving workloads to Azure versus keeping them on-premises.

U

Uptime:

The measure of system availability, typically expressed as a percentage in SLA agreements.

V

Virtual Machine (VM):

An emulation of a physical computer in Azure that runs Windows or Linux, offering control over OS, storage, and installed software.

Virtual Network (VNet):

A fundamental building block for private networking in Azure that enables secure communication among resources.

W

Web App (App Service):

A PaaS offering in Azure that allows for hosting web applications, RESTful APIs, and mobile backends with built-in scaling and patching.

Well-Architected Framework:

Microsoft's guidance for designing secure, high-performing, resilient, and efficient cloud applications.

Summary

This glossary provides foundational definitions for the key concepts, services, and terms featured in the AZ-900 certification exam and referenced throughout this guide. You can use it as a quick review tool before your exam or as a reference when revisiting specific chapters.

Tip: Bookmark or print this glossary. Familiarity with terminology will reduce hesitation and confusion during the exam and reinforce your understanding in future Azure-related roles or certifications.

Resources for Further Learning

Completing your AZ-900 preparation is just the beginning of a broader journey into cloud computing. While this book has equipped you with the foundational concepts, terminology, and practical skills necessary to pass the Microsoft Azure Fundamentals exam, continuous learning is essential for staying up-to-date with a rapidly evolving cloud ecosystem.

This section provides an extensive catalog of learning resources, tools, platforms, communities, and certifications that will help you deepen your Azure expertise. Whether you're preparing for a more advanced certification like AZ-104, AZ-204, or exploring specialized domains like security, AI, or DevOps, these resources will guide your next steps.

Microsoft Learn

Microsoft Learn is the official, self-paced learning platform offered by Microsoft. It provides:

- Modular content aligned with certifications
- Interactive labs and sandbox environments
- Built-in progress tracking and badges

Recommended AZ-900 Learning Path:

https://learn.microsoft.com/en-us/training/paths/azure-fundamentals/

This path includes the following modules:

- Describe cloud computing

- Describe core Azure services
- Describe Azure pricing and support
- Describe Azure governance and compliance

Features:

- Hands-on labs with sandbox environments (no subscription needed)
- Quizzes to reinforce understanding
- Bookmarking for future review

Official Microsoft Documentation

The **Microsoft Azure Documentation** portal is the authoritative reference for service specifications, architecture diagrams, quickstarts, and tutorials.

Portal:https://learn.microsoft.com/en-us/azure/

Use Cases:

- Reference syntax for CLI/PowerShell
- Understand service limits and region availability
- Deep dive into technical configuration

Pro Tip: Bookmark theWhat's New in Azure[10] page to stay updated on service changes and preview features.

---

10. https://azure.microsoft.com/en-us/updates/

Azure Certification Pathways

The AZ-900 is the foundational step in Microsoft's certification ecosystem. Below are common paths to follow based on your role:

Administrator Path:

- **AZ-104:** Azure Administrator Associate
- **AZ-500:** Azure Security Engineer Associate

Developer Path:

- **AZ-204:** Azure Developer Associate
- **AZ-400:** DevOps Engineer Expert

Architect Path:

- **AZ-305:** Azure Solutions Architect Expert

Specialty Certifications:

- **AI-900:** Azure AI Fundamentals
- **DP-900:** Azure Data Fundamentals
- **SC-900:** Microsoft Security, Compliance, and Identity Fundamentals

These certifications build on AZ-900 and go deeper into domain-specific skills.

Books and Study Guides

Recommended Titles:

- *Exam Ref AZ-900 Microsoft Azure Fundamentals* by Jim Cheshire (Microsoft Press)
- *Azure for Architects* by Ritesh Modi
- *Cloud Adoption Framework* (free eBook from Microsoft)

Each of these provides expanded perspectives, design strategies, and practice questions.

Practice Exams and Simulators

To simulate the actual test environment and improve familiarity with exam format, the following resources are highly recommended:

Microsoft Official Practice Tests:

- Available via MeasureUp or directly from Microsoft Learn.
- Features timed, randomized questions with explanations.

Additional Providers:

- Whizlabs: Practice tests + video content
- Tutorials Dojo: Scenario-based questions, review guides
- ExamTopics: Community-sourced questions and discussions

Pro Tip: Don't memorize questions—focus on **understanding** why each answer is correct or incorrect.

Azure Hands-On Labs and Sandboxes

For practical experience, the following platforms offer guided labs and challenge-based exercises:

Microsoft Hands-on Labs:

- https://microsoftlearning.github.io/AZ-900T0x-MicrosoftAzureFundamentals/

GitHub Repositories:

- Microsoft Learn content and hands-on exercises are often published on GitHub for customization.
- Example:https://github.com/MicrosoftLearning

Azure Dev/Test Subscription:

- Sign up for a **Microsoft Developer Program** to get access to a free Azure subscription for development use.

Community Forums and Blogs

Staying engaged with the community can enhance your learning through shared experiences and tips.

Forums:

- Microsoft Q&A:https://learn.microsoft.com/en-us/answers/
- Reddit: r/Azure and r/AzureCertification
- Stack Overflow (Azure tag)

Blogs:

- Azure Blog:https://azure.microsoft.com/en-us/blog/
- Microsoft Tech Community:https://techcommunity.microsoft.com/
- Thomas Maurer (Microsoft MVP):https://www.thomasmaurer.ch/

YouTube and Video Courses

Some learners prefer video content. These YouTube channels and platforms provide structured walkthroughs and demonstrations.

Free YouTube Channels:

- Microsoft Developer: Official Azure content and event recordings
- John Savill's Technical Training: Known for "Exam Cram" series
- FreeCodeCamp.org: Azure beginner videos

Paid Platforms:

- Pluralsight (Microsoft has partnered with them for Azure paths)
- LinkedIn Learning
- Udemy (look for AZ-900-specific courses with high ratings and recent updates)

Tools for Daily Practice

To build long-term fluency, incorporate the following into your routine:

- **Azure CLI**: Practice creating and managing resources
- **Bicep/ARM Templates**: Start with simple infrastructure as code examples
- **Azure Portal Dashboards**: Build a custom dashboard for visualizing services
- **Log Analytics and KQL (Kusto Query Language)**: Begin with basic queries

Example KQL Query:

```
AzureActivity
| where OperationName == "Create Resource"
| summarize count() by ResourceGroup
```

Azure Architecture Guidance

Once you're comfortable with the basics, explore architectural best practices:

- **Azure Well-Architected Framework**

https://learn.microsoft.com/en-us/azure/architecture/framework/

- **Microsoft Cloud Adoption Framework (CAF)**

https://learn.microsoft.com/en-us/azure/cloud-adoption-framework/

These guides offer blueprints, security models, cost optimization strategies, and governance advice.

Stay Informed and Connected

To maintain a long-term connection with the Azure ecosystem:

- Subscribe to the **Azure Newsletter**
- Attend **Microsoft Build**, **Ignite**, or local **Azure Meetups**
- Follow Azure MVPs and Microsoft engineers on Twitter/X and LinkedIn
- Join the **Azure Certification Study Group** on Tech Community

Summary

The AZ-900 exam is only the beginning of your cloud journey. By using the curated resources listed in this section—ranging from official documentation and video tutorials to practice exams and community engagement—you can reinforce your knowledge, explore new domains, and position yourself for advanced certifications and real-world Azure projects.

Key Takeaways:

- Microsoft Learn and Azure Docs are the primary study and reference platforms.
- Practice exams help bridge theory and exam readiness.
- Sandbox labs offer a safe space to experiment and make mistakes.
- Join communities to exchange ideas, resolve doubts, and stay motivated.

- Use your foundational knowledge from AZ-900 as a launchpad into deeper technical paths.

Continuous learning is the defining trait of every successful cloud professional. Choose your next milestone, and keep building.

Sample Projects and Code Snippets

Applying your knowledge through hands-on projects is the most effective way to reinforce core Azure concepts and prepare for real-world scenarios. While the AZ-900 exam does not require advanced coding skills, familiarity with Azure's tools, resource deployments, and service interactions using code significantly enhances your understanding of how cloud services are provisioned and managed. This section provides a collection of sample projects, configurations, and code snippets that bring Azure fundamentals to life, using Azure CLI, PowerShell, Bicep templates, and ARM templates.

These examples are designed for beginners and focus on reinforcing concepts such as IaaS and PaaS deployment, resource group management, storage provisioning, monitoring, identity control, and cost-conscious infrastructure planning.

Project 1: Deploy a Virtual Machine and Configure Auto-Shutdown

Objective: Create a Linux VM, apply a resource tag, and configure it to auto-shutdown daily to save costs.

Steps:

1. Create a resource group:

az group create \

—name vm-lab-rg \

—location eastus

1. Deploy a B1s-sized VM:

az vm create \

—name MyLinuxVM \

—resource-group vm-lab-rg \

—image UbuntuLTS \

—admin-username azureuser \

—generate-ssh-keys \

—size Standard_B1s

1. Enable auto-shutdown:

az vm auto-shutdown \

—resource-group vm-lab-rg \

—name MyLinuxVM \

—time 1900 \

—timezone "UTC"

1. Add a tag:

az resource tag \

—tags Environment=Lab Owner=student \

—ids $(az vm show—name MyLinuxVM—resource-group vm-lab-rg—query id -o tsv)

Project 2: Deploy a Static Website on Azure Blob Storage

Objective: Provision a storage account, enable static website hosting, upload content, and access the site via public URL.

Steps:

1. Create a resource group and storage account:

az group create—name storage-demo-rg—location westeurope

az storage account create \

—name mystaticwebdemo \

—resource-group storage-demo-rg \

—location westeurope \

—sku Standard_LRS \

—kind StorageV2 \

—enable-static-website true

1. Enable static site hosting and upload content:

az storage blob upload \

—account-name mystaticwebdemo \

—container-name '$web' \

—name index.html \

—file index.html \

—content-type text/html

1. Retrieve site URL:

az storage account show \

—name mystaticwebdemo \

—resource-group storage-demo-rg \

—query "primaryEndpoints.web" \

—output tsv

Project 3: Role Assignment for Azure Resource Group

Objective: Assign a user read-only access to a resource group using RBAC.

az role assignment create \

—assignee student@example.com \

—role Reader \

—resource-group vm-lab-rg

Explanation:

This applies least privilege principles, which is a core identity security strategy in Azure.

Project 4: Monitor Resources with Log Analytics

Workspace

Objective: Set up a Log Analytics workspace and link it to a VM for monitoring purposes.

1. Create the workspace:

az monitor log-analytics workspace create \

—resource-group vm-lab-rg \

—workspace-name vmInsightsWorkspace

1. Link workspace to VM:

az monitor diagnostic-settings create \

—resource $(az vm show—name MyLinuxVM—resource-group vm-lab-rg—query id -o tsv) \

—name diagSettings \

—workspace $(az monitor log-analytics workspace show—resource-group vm-lab-rg—workspace-name vmInsightsWorkspace—query id -o tsv) \

—metrics '[{"category":"AllMetrics","enabled":true}]' \

—logs '[{"category":"LinuxSyslog","enabled":true}]'

Project 5: Infrastructure as Code with Bicep

Objective: Deploy a storage account using Bicep.

File: storage.bicep

resource storage 'Microsoft.Storage/storageAccounts@2022-09-01' = {

name: 'mybicepstoragedemo'

location: resourceGroup().location

sku: {

name: 'Standard_LRS'

}

kind: 'StorageV2'

properties: {

accessTier: 'Hot'

}

}

Deploy using Azure CLI:

az deployment group create \

—resource-group storage-demo-rg \

—template-file storage.bicep

Project 6: Configure a Budget with Alerts

Objective: Set up a spending cap and email alerts using Azure Cost Management.

1. Create a budget:

```
az consumption budget create \
—amount 50 \
—time-grain monthly \
—name monthlyDevBudget \
—resource-group vm-lab-rg \
—category cost \
—start-date 2024-01-01 \
—end-date 2024-12-31 \
—notification emailAlert \
enabled=true \
operator=GreaterThan \
threshold=80 \
contact-emails student@example.com
```

Explanation:

This proactive measure ensures resource costs are monitored and users are alerted before the budget limit is reached.

Project 7: Deploy a Web App with Azure App Service

Objective: Create and deploy a basic web app using Azure App Service and App Service Plan.

```
az appservice plan create \
—name appserviceplan01 \
```

—resource-group vm-lab-rg \

—sku F1 \

—is-linux

az webapp create \

—resource-group vm-lab-rg \

—plan appserviceplan01 \

—name mywebappdemo01 \

—runtime "NODE|18-lts"

az webapp deployment source config-local-git \

—name mywebappdemo01 \

—resource-group vm-lab-rg

Result:

You receive a Git deployment URL to push your code directly to the app.

Project 8: Implement Azure Policy to Enforce Tags

Objective: Create a policy to enforce that all resources must have an 'Environment' tag.

az policy definition create \

—name enforceTag \

—display-name "Require Environment Tag" \

—description "Ensures all resources have the Environment tag" \

```
—rules '{
"if": {
"field": "[concat('tags[', parameters('tagName'), ']')]",
"exists": "false"
},
"then": {
"effect": "deny"
}
}' \
—params '{
"tagName": {
"type": "String",
"metadata": {
"description": "Name of the required tag",
"displayName": "Tag Name"
}
}
}' \
—mode Indexed
```

Apply the policy to a resource group or subscription afterward.

Summary

The sample projects and code snippets provided in this section offer practical reinforcement of concepts covered in the AZ-900 exam and throughout your Azure learning journey. They emphasize best practices around identity, cost management, deployment automation, and resource governance.

Key Takeaways:

- Experiment with CLI and Bicep to strengthen deployment fluency.
- Use tagging, budgets, and RBAC for governance and cost control.
- Apply security and monitoring features proactively using diagnostic settings and policies.
- Keep infrastructure modular and reusable using templates.

With these building blocks in place, you'll be well-equipped to scale your knowledge toward more advanced certifications, projects, and roles within the Azure ecosystem.

API Reference Guide

Understanding how to interact with Microsoft Azure through APIs is crucial for building automation, integrating services, and achieving full control over your cloud infrastructure programmatically. Although the AZ-900 exam does not require deep knowledge of APIs, a basic understanding of Azure REST APIs, SDKs, and command-line interface (CLI) endpoints provides valuable insight into how Azure services are managed behind the scenes.

This section offers a detailed overview of Azure APIs and programming interfaces, including REST, ARM (Azure Resource

Manager), CLI commands, and SDKs in various programming languages. By mastering these interfaces, you enable scalable deployments, automation strategies, and tighter integration between applications and Azure services.

Introduction to Azure APIs

Azure provides multiple layers of API access to manage and interact with cloud services:

- **Azure REST APIs** – Direct HTTP interface to Azure services
- **Azure Resource Manager (ARM) API** – Central to provisioning and managing Azure resources
- **Azure CLI and PowerShell** – Command-line tools built on top of ARM APIs
- **Azure SDKs** – Language-specific libraries for .NET, JavaScript, Python, Java, Go, and others

Each layer abstracts varying degrees of complexity and caters to different user preferences—whether you're a developer, system administrator, or DevOps engineer.

Azure REST API Overview

The **Azure REST API** is a set of endpoints that allow you to perform CRUD (Create, Read, Update, Delete) operations on nearly all Azure services.

Base URL Format:

https://management.azure.com/{resourcePath}?api-version={apiVersion}

Example – List Resource Groups:

GET https://management.azure.com/subscriptions/{subscriptionId}/resourcegroups?api-version=2021-04-01

Headers Required:

Authorization: Bearer <access_token>

Content-Type: application/json

Example Response:

{

"value": [

{

"id": "/subscriptions/.../resourceGroups/myResourceGroup",

"name": "myResourceGroup",

"location": "eastus",

"properties": {

"provisioningState": "Succeeded"

}

}

]

}

Authentication:

REST APIs use OAuth 2.0 tokens, typically acquired via Azure AD. You can authenticate using service principals or user accounts.

Use Cases:

- Automating resource creation from custom apps
- Integrating Azure into third-party CI/CD tools
- Querying subscription usage or diagnostic data

Azure Resource Manager (ARM) API

ARM is the **deployment and management layer** of Azure. It defines how all resources are structured, named, tagged, and deployed.

Common ARM API Endpoints:

Operation	REST Endpoint Format
Create Resource Group	PUT /subscriptions/{subId}/resourcegroups/{rgName}
List Resources	GET /subscriptions/{subId}/resources
Delete VM	DELETE /subscriptions/{subId}/resourceGroups/{rg}/providers/Microsoft.Compute/virtualMachines/{vmName}

ARM Templates are JSON-based definitions for declaratively deploying resources using these APIs.

Example ARM Template Snippet:

```
{
"type": "Microsoft.Compute/virtualMachines",
"apiVersion": "2021-11-01",
"name": "vmName",
```

```
"location": "eastus",

"properties": {

...

}

}
```

Deployment via REST:

PUT https://management.azure.com/subscriptions/{subId}/resourcegroups/{rgName}/providers/Microsoft.Resources/deployments/myDeployment?api-version=2021-04-01

Payload: ARM template + parameters.

Azure CLI (Command-Line Interface)

The **Azure CLI** is a cross-platform tool that allows you to interact with Azure services from the command line.

Installation:

curl -sL https://aka.ms/InstallAzureCLIDeb | sudo bash

Login:

az login

Common CLI Commands:

- List all VMs:

az vm list—output table

- Create a storage account:

az storage account create \

—name mystorage123 \

—resource-group demo-rg \

—location eastus \

—sku Standard_LRS

- Deploy a resource group template:

az deployment group create \

—resource-group demo-rg \

—template-file azuredeploy.json \

—parameters azuredeploy.parameters.json

Why Use CLI?

- Easier syntax than raw REST
- Ideal for scripting and DevOps pipelines
- Cross-platform and lightweight

Azure PowerShell

Azure PowerShell is a set of cmdlets for managing Azure resources from Windows, Linux, or macOS environments.

Login:

Connect-AzAccount

Common Cmdlets:

- Create a new resource group:

New-AzResourceGroup -Name demo-rg -Location "East US"

- Create a virtual network:

New-AzVirtualNetwork -Name vnet01 -ResourceGroupName demo-rg -Location "East US" -AddressPrefix "10.0.0.0/16"

PowerShell is often favored by Windows administrators and those already familiar with scripting in PowerShell.

Azure SDKs

Azure provides SDKs in multiple languages to allow developers to build native applications that interact with Azure services.

Supported Languages:

- .NET
- Java
- Python
- JavaScript/TypeScript (Node.js and browser)
- Go
- C++

Install (Python Example):

pip install azure-mgmt-resource

Sample Python Code:

```
from azure.identity import DefaultAzureCredential

from azure.mgmt.resource import ResourceManagementClient

credential = DefaultAzureCredential()

subscription_id = 'your-subscription-id'

client = ResourceManagementClient(credential, subscription_id)

client.resource_groups.create_or_update(

"example-rg",

{"location": "eastus"}

)
```

Use Cases:

- Automating deployments within application code
- Integrating Azure services directly into backend applications
- Managing Azure resources programmatically

Azure Graph API

The **Microsoft Graph API** allows you to access Microsoft 365 services, including Azure AD.

Example – Get Azure AD Users:

```
GET https://graph.microsoft.com/v1.0/users

Authorization: Bearer <access_token>
```

Graph API is useful for managing identity-related services like users, groups, roles, and sign-in logs.

API Testing Tools

To explore and test Azure REST APIs, use:

- **Postman** – Ideal for sending authenticated API calls
- **curl** – Lightweight command-line HTTP client
- **Insomnia** – Developer-friendly GUI alternative to Postman
- **Swagger UI** – Available for many Azure services (e.g., Cognitive Services)

API Security Considerations

- **Use managed identities** to avoid embedding credentials
- **Apply RBAC** to control API access scopes
- **Use HTTPS** for all interactions
- **Set up API throttling and alerts** to detect abuse or overuse
- **Use Azure Key Vault** to store secrets and API keys

Summary

Azure APIs form the backbone of all programmatic interactions with the cloud. Whether you're building internal tools, integrating services, or automating deployments, understanding these APIs—and how they relate to Azure CLI, ARM, and SDKs—is vital for real-world cloud proficiency.

Key Takeaways:

- REST and ARM APIs offer granular, flexible control but require authentication and correct versioning.

- Azure CLI and PowerShell abstract API calls into user-friendly commands.
- SDKs enable deep service integration in popular programming languages.
- APIs should be accessed securely using tokens, managed identities, and encrypted channels.
- Testing and documentation tools help validate and explore APIs interactively.

Mastering Azure's API surface area enables seamless automation, faster deployments, and future-ready architecture—all essential skills for evolving beyond AZ-900 and into advanced Azure roles and projects.

Frequently Asked Questions

This final section compiles a comprehensive list of frequently asked questions (FAQs) regarding the AZ-900: Microsoft Azure Fundamentals certification, exam logistics, cloud concepts, Azure services, and practical scenarios. These questions are based on real-world candidate experiences, Microsoft documentation, and the most common concerns expressed by learners during their certification journey.

Whether you're planning your exam, troubleshooting subscription access, or clarifying ambiguous topics, this reference aims to provide fast, reliable answers and eliminate uncertainty before test day.

General Certification Questions

Q: Is the AZ-900 certification mandatory to pursue higher-level Azure certifications?

A: No. AZ-900 is not a prerequisite for other certifications. However, it provides a foundational understanding that is highly recommended before attempting Associate- or Expert-level exams (e.g., AZ-104, AZ-305).

Q: How long is the AZ-900 certification valid?

A: As of 2023, AZ-900 certifications do not expire. However, always confirm with the latest Microsoft certification policies on their Learn portal.

Q: What is the format of the AZ-900 exam?

A: Multiple-choice, multi-select, yes/no, drag-and-drop, hot areas, and case-based questions. There are 40–60 questions, and the passing score is 700 out of 1000.

Q: How much does the exam cost?

A: Pricing varies by region. In the UK, it's approximately £69; in the US, about $99. Always verify on Microsoft's official registration page.

Q: How do I register for the exam?

A: Visit:https://learn.microsoft.com/en-us/certifications/exams/az-900/

You can register via Pearson VUE for online or in-person proctored delivery.

Study and Preparation Questions

Q: How long should I study for the AZ-900 exam?

A: On average, 1–2 weeks of focused study (15–20 total hours) is sufficient if you follow a structured path like Microsoft Learn or this guide. Beginners may need more time.

Q: Is hands-on experience required to pass AZ-900?

A: No, but it's highly recommended. While the exam is theoretical, hands-on familiarity with the Azure Portal and CLI enhances understanding and retention.

Q: What is the best way to prepare for the exam?

A: Combine:

- Microsoft Learn modules
- Practice tests (Whizlabs, MeasureUp)
- This study guide's hands-on labs and glossary
- Azure free tier usage

Q: Does Microsoft offer any free resources or vouchers?

A: Yes. Occasionally, Microsoft offers free exam vouchers through live virtual training events. Check the Microsoft Events page or Tech Community for upcoming opportunities.

Exam-Day and Delivery Questions

Q: What ID do I need to take the exam online?

A: A government-issued photo ID (passport, driver's license). Ensure your name matches your Microsoft profile exactly.

Q: Can I use notes or resources during the exam?

A: No. The AZ-900 is closed-book. Online proctoring includes system monitoring and camera verification.

Q: What if I lose internet connection during the online exam?

A: If your session drops, you can usually reconnect. If you can't resume, contact Pearson VUE for assistance. Rescheduling may be necessary in rare cases.

Q: How soon do I get my result?

A: Immediately after the exam. A digital score report is provided. The official badge appears on your Microsoft Certification Dashboard within 48 hours.

Azure Concepts and Services FAQs

Q: What's the difference between Azure AD and Active Directory?

A: Azure AD is the cloud-based identity service used for SaaS and Azure resources. Windows AD (on-premises) manages traditional IT infrastructure. Azure AD supports modern protocols like OAuth2 and SAML.

Q: Can a single resource belong to multiple resource groups?

A: No. Each resource belongs to exactly one resource group at a time. You can, however, move resources between groups.

Q: What's the difference between Regions and Availability Zones?

A: A **region** is a geographic area with at least one datacenter. **Availability Zones** are physically separate datacenters within a region, offering high availability and fault tolerance.

Q: How are IaaS, PaaS, and SaaS different in Azure?

A:

- **IaaS:** Full control over infrastructure (e.g., Azure VMs)
- **PaaS:** Focus on app deployment, Azure handles OS and runtime (e.g., Azure App Service)
- **SaaS:** Fully managed applications (e.g., Microsoft 365)

Q: What happens when I stop a VM?

A:

- **Stopped (allocated):** VM is off, but you're still charged for reserved compute resources
- **Deallocated:** VM is off, resources released—no compute charges apply

---

Cost Management and Billing FAQs

Q: Is Azure's Free Tier really free?

A: Yes, if you stay within the limits. The free tier includes:

- $200 credit for the first 30 days
- 12 months of free services (e.g., B1S VM, 5GB Blob Storage)
- Always-free services (e.g., Azure Functions, Event Grid under quota)

Q: How can I avoid surprise billing?

A:

- Set up **budgets** and **alerts**
- Use **resource tagging** to monitor by project
- **Deallocate** VMs when not in use
- **Delete unused resources** (especially disks and IPs)

Q: What is the Azure Pricing Calculator used for?

A: It estimates monthly costs based on selected services and configurations. Ideal for planning projects before deployment.

Role-Based Access and Security Questions

Q: What is RBAC and how does it differ from IAM?

A: RBAC (Role-Based Access Control) is Azure's model for granting access to users based on assigned roles. IAM (Identity and Access Management) is a broader category that includes RBAC, authentication, and policy enforcement.

Q: Can I assign roles to groups?

A: Yes. Assigning RBAC roles to Azure AD groups is a best practice for managing large user bases.

Q: What is a Managed Identity?

A: A system-assigned identity for an Azure resource (like a VM) that allows it to authenticate with other services (e.g., Key Vault) without credentials.

Governance and Compliance FAQs

Q: What is Azure Policy?

A: Azure Policy enforces rules and effects over resources. For example, requiring that all resources have a specific tag or blocking certain SKUs from being deployed.

Q: How does Azure help with compliance requirements?

A: Azure provides tools like:

- Compliance Manager
- Microsoft Trust Center
- Audit logs via Azure Monitor and Security Center

Azure also maintains certifications for GDPR, ISO, HIPAA, and more.

Miscellaneous and Best Practices

Q: Can I rename a resource group in Azure?

A: No. Resource groups cannot be renamed. To simulate a rename, create a new one and move resources manually.

Q: What is Azure Marketplace?

A: An online store of preconfigured software and service templates offered by Microsoft and third-party vendors, deployable directly into your Azure environment.

Q: Should I use the Azure CLI or PowerShell?

A: Depends on your background. CLI is generally simpler and cross-platform. PowerShell is preferred for Windows admins or existing PowerShell scripts.

Q: What's the easiest way to get started with Azure automation?

A: Start with:

- Azure CLI scripts
- ARM or Bicep templates
- Azure Automation for schedule-based workflows

Summary

These FAQs aim to address the most relevant, recurring questions from candidates and new Azure users. Use this section to revisit key concepts, validate assumptions, and reinforce your understanding before and after taking the AZ-900 exam.

Key Takeaways:

- AZ-900 is accessible, but preparation should be deliberate and hands-on.
- Always stay informed via Microsoft Learn, documentation, and community forums.
- Clarify tricky concepts like resource groups, identity, and pricing early.
- Treat FAQs as checkpoints—if any answer here surprises you, revisit that topic.

With this reference at hand, your path to passing AZ-900 and confidently engaging with Microsoft Azure is clearer, structured, and achievable.

www.ingramcontent.com/pod-product-compliance
Lightning Source LLC
LaVergne TN
LVHW090308210926
848480LV00001B/168
9798231875924